MW01405631

Call Him Mac

GARY L. STUART
FOREWORD BY MICHAEL DALY HAWKINS

CALL HIM MAC

Ernest W. McFarland, the Arizona Years

SENTINEL PEAK
TUCSON

SENTINEL PEAK
An imprint of The University of Arizona Press
www.uapress.arizona.edu

© 2018 by Gary L. Stuart
All rights reserved. Published 2018

ISBN-13: 978-1-941451-06-9 (cloth)
ISBN-13: 978-1-941451-05-2 (paper)

Cover design by Leigh McDonald
Cover photo: Ernest W. McFarland at his trial bench, 1935. Arizona State Library, Archives and Public Records, History and Archives Division, #12-0025

All photographs are courtesy of the McFarland family.

Publication of this book was made possible in part by funding from the McFarland Historical State Park Advisory Committee, Inc., an Arizona nonprofit corporation, and by Kara Lynne Lewis, William Craig Lewis, John David Lewis, Delbert Lewis Jr., and Leah Lewis.

Library of Congress Cataloging-in-Publication Data
Names: Stuart, Gary L., 1939– author. | Hawkins, Michael Daly, 1945– writer of foreword.
Title: Call him Mac : Ernest W. McFarland, the Arizona years / Gary L. Stuart ; foreword by Michael Daly Hawkins.
Description: Tucson : The University of Arizona Press, 2018. | Includes bibliographical references and index.
Identifiers: LCCN 2018009210| ISBN 9781941451069 (cloth : alk. paper) | ISBN 9781941451052 (pbk. : alk. paper)
Subjects: LCSH: McFarland, Ernest William, 1894–1984. | Governors—Arizona—Biography. | Judges—Arizona—Biography. | LCGFT: Biographies.
Classification: LCC F815.3.M34 S78 2018 | DDC 979.1/053092 [B] —dc23 LC record available at https://lccn.loc.gov/2018009210

Printed in the United States of America
♾ This paper meets the requirements of ANSI/NISO Z39.48-1992 (Permanence of Paper).

Contents

	Foreword by Michael Daly Hawkins	vii
	Chronology	ix
	Prologue	3
1.	Mac: Sooner Born and Sooner Bred, 1894	7
2.	Mac Joins the U.S. Navy, 1917	14
3.	Mac Moves to Phoenix, 1919	19
4.	Mac: Law, Political Science, and Sociology, 1919	21
5.	Mac and Florence, Arizona, 1924	26
6.	Mac Becomes a Lawyer, 1921	33
7.	Mac Runs for Pinal County Attorney, 1924	38
8.	Mac and Tommy Fulbright, 1929	41
9.	Mac and the Eva Dugan Case, 1930	50
10.	Mac, Clare, and Their Children, 1925 to 1929	56
11.	Mac and Henry Fountain Ashurst in the 1930s	67
12.	Mac and the Winnie Ruth Judd Case, 1933	73
13.	Mac Runs for Pinal County Judge Twice, 1930 and 1934	83
14.	Mac and Edna, 1939	87
15.	Mac and Henry Fountain Ashurst, 1940	90

16.	Mac's Primary Campaign Against Henry Fountain Ashurst, 1940	97
17.	Mac's Retail Politics, 1940	105
18.	Mac's General Election Campaign for the U.S. Senate, 1940	125
19.	Mac Goes to Washington, DC, December 1940	137
20.	Mac on the Cusp of the U.S. Senate, 1940	139
21.	Mac as Senator, 1941 to 1952	145
22.	Mac and Barry Goldwater, 1952	150
23.	Mac, 1954 to 1964: Governor, Businessman, Lawyer, Farmer, Grandfather	156
24.	Mac and the Arizona Supreme Court, 1964	160
25.	Mac's Grandchildren	168
26.	Mac and KTVK, 1971	177
27.	Mac's Memorial at the State Capitol, 1998 and 2015	181
	Epilogue, 2017	183
	Finis Mac	193
	Acknowledgments	*195*
	Notes	*197*
	Bibliography	*203*
	Index	*205*

Foreword

This is a book about a man who literally could not keep a job: small-town lawyer, county prosecutor, state trial judge, U.S. senator, governor, state supreme court justice. At every stage of that progression, Ernest W. McFarland insisted that he be called simply "Mac." (And who am I to call him anything but.) Mac gave no one he came in contact with the impression that he was different from any of them, yet he was a highly educated law and political science graduate of Stanford, conversant, before ever holding public office, in the details of everything from water law to the initiative and referendum process. Mac felt the highs and lows of seeking and retaining public office—from his stunning 1940 upset of Senator Henry Fountain Ashurst to his 1952 loss to a then relatively unknown Phoenix City Councilman Barry Goldwater, a loss magnified by Mac's position at the time as U.S. Senate majority leader. He also demonstrated an incredible ability to rebound from defeat: just two years later, Arizona voters put him in the governor's chair for two terms. Then, following a second loss to Senator Goldwater in 1958, the voters put Mac on the Arizona Supreme Court, where his colleagues eventually made him chief justice. Mac was not just a title holder; his hardscrabble Oklahoma upbringing and his World War I naval service, where he very nearly perished from pneumonia, made him a natural consensus builder and hard worker. In the U.S. Senate, he was instrumental in the creation of the GI Bill, which gave millions of returning service members a chance at a higher education and a ticket into the middle class—easily the most successful social experiment of the twentieth century. As governor, he led efforts to revise the tax code in ways that spawned the development of high-tech industries from the Sperry Rand Corporation of Mac's day to the Intel of today. The state park system was established during his term, and state aid to K–12 public education substantially increased.

This book is not the first effort to characterize the life of this remarkable man. Mac's own autobiography was published in 1979, and James E. McMillan Jr. produced a 618-page full biography, titled *Ernest W. McFarland: Majority Leader of the United States Senate, Governor and Chief Justice of the State of Arizona*, in 2004. What Gary Stuart does in this book in the pages that follow is not only build on what has existed before, but he also gives the reader a remarkable insight into the background and development of one of Arizona's most remarkable public figures—someone whose career rose like a comet only to crash to earth and then rebound to cast a bright light on his adopted state in a way that no one, before or since, has been able to capture. Gary undertook this effort at the urging of and with support of Mac's grandchildren. We should all be grateful to both for the result.

—*Michael Daly Hawkins, 2018*

Chronology

1894	Born October 9, near Earlsboro, Oklahoma
1914	Graduates, Earlsboro High School
1915	Graduates, East Central Normal School, Ada, Oklahoma
1917	Bachelor's degree, University of Oklahoma at Norman
1917	Joins U.S. Navy, assigned to Great Lakes Naval School, Illinois
1919	Honorable discharge, U.S. Navy
1919	Moves to Phoenix, Arizona
1919	Enrolls, Stanford University
1921	Admitted to Arizona Bar
1921	Opens law practice, Casa Grande, Arizona
1922	Juris Doctorate, Stanford Law School
1923	Appointed an Arizona assistant attorney general
1924	Elected Pinal County attorney, moves to Florence, Arizona
1925	Marries Clare Collins Smith
1927	Son, William Ernest McFarland II, born
1929	Daughter, Jean Clare, born
1929	Both children die
1930	Prosecutes and upholds Eva Dugan's death sentence. She is decapitated at her hanging.
1930	Defeated at first run for election as Pinal County superior court judge
1930	Loses wife, Clare, and their newborn baby, Juliet, to complications of child birth

1931	Continues private law practice in Florence, Arizona
1933	Represents Winnie Ruth Judd during her insanity defense, saves her from death penalty
1934	Elected Pinal County superior court judge
1935	Meets and courts Edna Eveland Smith
1936	Issues Gila River Water Rights decree
1939	Marries Edna Eveland Smith
1940	Defeats Henry Fountain Ashurst in Democratic primary election for U.S. Senate
1940	Defeats Irving A. Jennings in general election for U.S. Senate
1941	Sworn in as junior U.S. senator with Senator Carl Hayden
1944	Writes and co-authors GI Bill, House passes bill, FDR signs bill into law
1946	Declines offer by President Truman to appointment as federal judge in Arizona
1946	Re-elected to U.S. Senate
1948	Declines overtures to run with Truman for vice president of United States, also declines to take a seat on U.S. Supreme Court
1950	Becomes acting majority leader in U.S. Senate
1951	Selected majority leader in U.S. Senate, chooses Lyndon Baines Johnson as assistant majority leader, "whip"
1951	Daughter Jewell McFarland marries Delbert Lewis. They will give Mac five grandchildren: Kara (April 11, 1954); William (September 24, 1957); John (May 9, 1960); Leah (July 18, 1966); and Delbert Jr., (May 3, 1967).
1952	Defeated by Barry Goldwater for U.S. Senate
1953	Founds Arizona Television Company (KTVK) in Phoenix Elected to Western Union, Inc., board of directors
1954	Elected as Arizona governor
1955	Delivers oral argument in U.S. Supreme Court in Central Arizona Project lawsuit against California
1956	Elected to second term as Arizona governor
1958	Defeated by Barry Goldwater for U.S. Senate
1959	Returns to private law practice in Florence and runs Arizona Channel 3 in Phoenix
1964	Elected as associate justice, Arizona Supreme Court
1965	Writes opinion in *Miranda v. Arizona*
1966	*Miranda* decision overturned by U.S. Supreme Court, establishing *Miranda* rules regarding unwarned confessions
1967	Selected as vice chief justice, Arizona Supreme Court
1968	Selected as chief justice, Arizona Supreme Court

1971	Retires from Arizona Supreme Court and public life, but continues leadership roles in his TV companies
1979	Writes autobiography: *Mac: The Autobiography of Ernest W. McFarland*
1980	Designated as Stanford Law School's "Most Distinguished Living Alumnus"
1984	Dies of heart failure in Phoenix. Lies in state under Capitol Dome and interred at Greenwood Memorial Cemetery

CALL HIM MAC

Prologue

This book is about a teacher, lawyer, judge, and a United States senator. A governor, supreme court justice, and an entrepreneur. He had titles, accolades, comrades in arms, and a principled, highly nuanced view of the world. His friends numbered in the tens of thousands. They were real friends—not virtual or digital—just old-fashioned analog friends. His were the kind that broke their necks getting to one another's funerals. Except for his parents, everyone else called him "Mac." He insisted on that.

Born in a log cabin near Earlsboro, Oklahoma, on the Pottawatomie Strip, he thought his home was the western frontier. And for him, it was. The day of his birth, October 9, 1894, was also in the year that Coca-Cola was sold in bottles for the first time; it became Mac's favorite soft drink. That was also the year the Ohio national guard killed three white men in the process of lynching a black man. The black man was rescued; Mac would have been proud of that. Kipling wrote *The Jungle Book*, a book Mac loved. Great Britain introduced "death duties," which became inheritance taxes in the United States, something Mac approved of as an organizing principle.

But in all of America, from then to now, Mac was the only person to ever serve his country during time of war, serve his state as a prosecutor and as a defense lawyer, be elected to the supreme court of his state, then be elected in a landslide to the U.S. Senate (where he would become the majority leader), be elected governor of his state, and finally serve as chief justice of the Arizona Supreme Court.

Mac was born at the end of the nineteenth century but lived most of his life in the twentieth. In telling his Arizona story, it seems appropriate to contrast the elemental differences between the century of his birth and that of his death. The nineteenth century is best known for what collapsed; the Spanish, Napoleonic, Holy Roman, and Mughal empires imploded. While the American experience was stretching its legs, the British Empire was virtually unchallenged in world dominance after 1815—the Napoleonic Wars. With that calamity, the Pax Britannica ushered in globalization, industrialization, and economic integration on a massive scale. It's fair to say that none of the pioneering families in Oklahoma or Arizona knew of Pax Britannica.

The twentieth century was about constant renewal. The first global-scale wars between world powers across continents and oceans spawned in World Wars I and II. Nationalism became a major political issue in the world in the twentieth century. The right of nations to self-determination came with official decolonization. The century was dominated by existential changes in politics, ideology, economics, society, culture, science, technology, and medicine. Arguably, there was more technological and scientific progress in the twentieth century than in all other centuries combined since the dawn of civilization. Terms like ideology, world war, genocide, and nuclear war entered common usage. Einstein's theory of relativity and the new quantum physics profoundly changed physical science, forcing scientists and politicians to accept a universe much more complex than previously believed. It was a century that began with horses, simple automobiles, and freighters, but ended with high-speed rail, cruise ships, global commercial air travel, space shuttles, the Internet, and states colored red or blue. Mac grew up in that transitional period of explosive knowledge.

His rise from rural law practice in small-town Florence, Arizona, to the august position of majority leader in the U.S. Senate is well documented. He was proud of his Oklahoma birthplace, but his seasoning, leavening, and intellectual grasp came from Arizona. He was a political star in Washington, DC, but rural Arizona prepared him for every legislative mountain he climbed. He was a man of the people, by the people, and for the people. Today's politicians all use that cliché. Mac really was that man.

His political accomplishments are documented and archived in scores of state and national libraries. *What* he did is well known. But *how* Arizona's citizens and the state's culture shaped Mac is this book's previously untold story. It explains the fame that Mac created, not for himself, but for the thousands he served in Arizona and millions more by his unparalleled success in governance and statesmanship at the highest possible levels. His early Arizona story is a switchboard to past, present, and future big ideas.

Dr. J. E. Wallace Sterling, president emeritus of Stanford University, remembered him this way: "A boyhood on the frontier, naval service in World War I, a lawyer, attorney general, senator, governor, chief justice! Who else has had such a varied and distinguished career; who else such a range of public service . . . He could count friends in the tens of thousands from all walks of life who paid him the respect he so richly deserves, and who call him 'Mac.'"

Mac's principal biographer, Dr. James Elton McMillan Jr., captured Mac's sine qua non in his 2004 masterwork *Ernest W. McFarland: Majority Leader of the United States Senate, Governor and Chief Justice of the State of Arizona*. McMillan's exhaustive biography is historical prose. It is an accurate tome documenting Mac's service in the highest positions in the legislative, executive, and judicial branches of government. His record is unsurpassed in American political history. He was, as McMillan reported, also a "respected legal counselor, an honored television executive, a prosperous farmer, a writer, an advocate of historical preservation, a generous philanthropist, and a doting grandfather."

Another noted U.S. senator from Arizona, the Honorable Dennis DeConcini, said, "[He was] truly a man of the people. Perhaps the proof of which is that all who met him, from presidents to paupers, knew him simply as Mac."

Mac endured more than his share of life's tragedies. His first wife, Clare, died in 1930, shortly after the tragic deaths of their three young children. Mac married Edna in 1939 and adopted her daughter, Jewell. In 1951, Jewell married a young man from Florence, Arizona, named Delbert Lewis, and together they had five children; Kara, Bill, John, Leah, and Del Jr. Jewell became one of Arizona's most beloved philanthropists. She and her children doted on Mac, and they became the center of his life once he left politics behind.

This book, commissioned by his grandchildren, who loved him deeply, is Mac's personal story. It is not offered as strictly biography, but rather as the untold story of *how* Mac became Mac in Arizona. It is also Jewell's story. Mac adored Jewell and her children. He was twenty-five years old when he first moved to Arizona and forty-six when he left for Washington, DC. He came as Ernest, but left as Mac. Jewell went to the Capitol with Mac, and like her famous father, she became part of an Arizona legend. That took some doing. Here's how it happened.

1

Mac

Sooner Born and Sooner Bred, 1894

The old saying *Like father, like son* applies to William Thomas McFarland and his famous son, Earnest William McFarland. Mac's dad, a Tennessee farmer, married his mother, Keziah Smith, on December 1, 1881. They moved to Oklahoma in December 1891, a true pioneering family. Mac was born in Earlsboro, Oklahoma, on October 9, 1894. Oklahoma's rich history is deeply steeped in its homesteading families. Mac's family fit the typical frontier profile; it contained a big-boned, shaggy father, a determined wife, and several small children. The family arrived in Oklahoma in a prairie schooner bulging with chickens, farm implements, furniture, mattresses, and the ubiquitous family dog. A leather trunk and a few wooden boxes held mementos of past and perhaps happier days, a few worn books, some fragile china, and a bit of wedding lace.[1]

Mac inherited his father's genetic disposition toward an agricultural livelihood based on mobility, optimism, and a wandering eye to the west of wherever he was. His parents and older siblings, Forrest and Etta Pearl, moved by covered wagon from Tennessee to Texas to Oklahoma. The last move, three years before Mac was born, was timed to take full advantage of the now famous Pottawatomie Strip land run on September 22, 1891. That scene has been depicted many times on large and small American screens.

But Mac's parents and older siblings lived it. Prospective landowners lined up on a well-marked starting line waiting for a uniform signal, all with pioneering blood, stamina, and an eye for a better future. They readied themselves on horses and oxen, aboard carriages and buggies. It was widely reported that a few made the run on bicycle, and a handful were barefooted.

The enormous strip of land available for this famous run was what the federal government called, "previously unassigned tribal lands." That quaint phrase was code to avoid the plain truth. That strip of land had been continuously occupied for hundreds of years by the Pottawatomie, Shawnee, Iowa, Sac, and Fox Native American tribes. All had been subjugated by the U.S. Army. Now, white pilgrims and settlers were encouraged to make a run for these prime acres. They had to pay a small fee to file a claim to a quarter section of land: $1.25 per acre or $200.00 for a quarter section—160 acres. Twenty thousand people made the run that day; Mac's dad was near the front of the line. Only a fraction of the runners would ever file a claim. The race went to the swift and crafty because there were three times as many runners as there were claimable sections of land. The total acreage available that summer day was 1,120,000 acres. When settled, it populated a good part of south central Oklahoma. All of the new residents were white settlers from north, south, and east of Oklahoma. Few, if any, came from the American Southwest.

During the nineteenth century, many thousands of Native Americans were expelled from their ancestral homelands across North America and transported to the area including and surrounding present-day Oklahoma. The Choctaw was the first of the Five Civilized Tribes to be removed from the southeastern United States. The phrase *Trail of Tears* originated from a description of the removal of the Choctaw Nation in 1831, although the term is usually used for the Cherokee removal. The U.S. government deported seventeen thousand Cherokees and two thousand of their black slaves. The area, already occupied by Osage and Quapaw tribes, was initially called the Choctaw Nation. By 1890, the year before the famous Pottawatomie Strip land run was held, more than thirty Native American nations and tribes had been concentrated on land within Indian territory, which was then called "Indian Country."

William Thomas McFarland made the run by himself in a covered wagon. Because speed was essential, he had only what was vital to staking a winning claim—pick, hammer, saw, axe, shovel, and wood boards for marking the boundaries of his claim. He brought weapons to fend or fight off any who tried to claim his staked-out area. Those who took off early were called "sooners." Mac's family history records confirm he had to buy off one sooner, who had jumped the gun signal, for one hundred dollars.[2] William McFarland staked his 160-acre claim barely a half mile west of the Seminole Nation border. It was green fertile land graced by creeks flowing south to the Canadian River. This part of Oklahoma was atypical because it had an abundance of wood and water. Mac was born on that land, October 9, 1894, in the log cabin his father built. That allowed him to truthfully make the Lincolnesque political claim to a log-cabin birth. He could also claim the title of being the first native-born Oklahoman to serve in the United States Senate. He honed his farming skills on those 160 acres and rode plow and working horses, perhaps all the while nurturing the notion that his place in history would be farther west—on the western frontier—the Arizona territory.

Mac's father taught him many things. The ways of woodlands, flowing creeks and streams, wild and domestic animals, and hard work were Mac's boyhood. As the son of a prairie farmer, he hand-plowed furrows of cotton; later, Mac would do that again in Pinal County Arizona. He learned about the habits, care, and tending of horses. In the late 1930s, Mac would teach his daughter, Jewell, those same skills. The work was hard, seasonal, and constructive. He ate what his family produced; no more, no less. It was how his family got by, how they prospered. And it was how he would later use the habits of industry and steadfastness to his political advantage.

In time, Mac would gain national fame as a "workhorse senator, governor, and supreme court justice." He earned that reputation by first working with his hands in hard construction work and later by his hard political work. In any case, walking behind a plow and making straight furrows was as natural to Mac as breathing was. He would prove that in the 1940 race for the U.S. Senate seat, at that time held by the famous Henry Fountain Ashurst.

Mac, the third of five children, felt the physical demands of all sons of prairie farmers in the Midwest at the turn of the nineteenth century. They rode horseback through prairies, tended scattered beef and dairy cattle, dug fence postholes, and harvested plants and trees. Farm families were self-sufficient in the extreme—they built their own houses, stables, barns, and

Mac's Oklahoma family, ca. 1900.

storm cellars. William, the father, and Keziah, the mother, looked very much the part in old family photographs eventually collected by the McFarland and Lewis families in Arizona.

McMillan, the family historian and biographer, pored over those photographs and provided clear images. William stands out as tall, thin to an extreme, beardless with a paintbrush mustache, and a long narrow head set off by the McFarland ears, seemingly readying for flight. Like her husband, Keziah appears stern and judgmental, with a narrow-set mouth and deep, sharp eyes. Mac's older brother, Forrest, then twenty years old, was a mirror image of his father. Sixteen-year-old Etta Pearl added softness and beauty to the family photo. Mac, then known as Ernest, was just thirteen, and looked very much the freckle-faced lad. He seems uncomfortable in his homespun suit, being forced to pose. His eagerness to spring back out into the fields and streams with his ever-present shepherd dog running at his side is apparent. The youngest, a boy named Sterling Carl, was seven, wearing children's shorts, barefooted, but ready to either pose, or play.

Mac graduated from Earlsboro High School in 1914; he was twenty years old. Like many farming families, Mac's parents insisted he finish high school, even though he missed one year, while the family worked a different farm thirty miles farther north in a town called Okemah, a town too small to have a high school. Neither of Mac's parents were educated past the eighth grade, but they insisted that all five of their children graduate high school. Mac ranked third in his class with excellent grades in literature, physics, mathematics, history, Latin, and German. As he frequently told audiences in later years, graduating third in the class sounds great except for the fact that his school only had three graduates that year.

He led the insular life of all adults and children who farmed the vast prairies in south central Oklahoma at the turn of the nineteenth century. He met very few people, almost none of whom were his own age, traveled only in a small geographic circle, and was the epitome of a "quiet country boy bent on getting an education."[3] Higher education would, in just the next ten years, fundamentally change Mac. It truly was an "insular" way to live because farming people, at that time in that part of the world, focused narrowly on survival. They were insular, as in "stubbornly insular farming people." They worked from dawn to dusk on their own land, rarely traveled, and knew only village rural people in south central Oklahoma. Mac, understandably, knew only his own experience. But thanks to his decisions about higher education and where to start a new life, Mac became the epitome of a broad-minded, tolerant person. And he became a Democrat like his parents, aunts, and uncles.

After high school, Mac went to college at East Central Normal School (ECNS), which was renamed East Central University in 1985. There, he joined the Phi Delta Debating Club and became a public speaker, a job he took very seriously. His school records document he completed "Lessons in Vocal Expression, Processes of Thinking in the Modulation of the Voice, and the Speaking Voice—Principles of Training Simplified and Condensed." His boyhood school books survived his travels west, back east, and then back west. They are now archived among the 174 linear feet of boxes known as the McFarland Collection.[4] He moved beyond his hometown colloquial vernacular and became an accomplished public speaker early in life. His college classmate, Robert S. Kerr, an Oklahoman who would join Mac in the U.S. Senate in 1948, remembers predicting while they were both young men at ECNS that, "[Mac] likes to fight, and this spirit will likely lead him into politics. Once in, we venture that he will not stop before adding to his name M.C. or U.S.S."[5]

Mac's East Central 1915 college yearbook humorously, albeit inaccurately, predicts his postcollege years:

> Following the bent of his reckless disposition, Ernest becomes an aviator, and his heedless sense of adventure inspires him with the desire to circumnavigate the globe in twenty-four hours. This experiment leaves him hanging in the pines of the Rockies. Thereafter, McFarland is more conservative in his ideas, and he becomes the head of a small parish in Arkansas.[6]

Fortunately, Mac's yearbook prediction was wrong. His college years resulted in his vacillation between recklessness and conservatism. He once got tricked into getting drunk with classmates and enjoyed it. But he also learned from it. He listened and experimented with both sides of many personal and political issues. He articulated eloquently. Those skills would later serve him and the state of Arizona well as he developed remarkable political skills, friends, voters, and a national reputation.

When he graduated college, he earned a teaching certificate and took a position at the crossroads town called Schoolton, on the northern tip of Seminole County. He was a teacher on horseback. Some town rowdies tried to run him off, but his newfound homespun humor and his speaking ability put them off their game. By then, he was also a man of considerable physical presence. These developing traits would serve him well in both negotiation and compromise in the U.S. Senate.[7]

While at his first teaching position, Mac became embroiled in a political controversy involving the ECNS president, Charles Briles. It grew out of an allegation that Briles gave preferential treatment to Methodists over Baptists. Briles was acquitted at trial,[8] but nonetheless, the political spoils cost Mac his teaching job and Briles his job as college president. The scandal caused Mac to reevaluate his career decisions, explaining, "I decided I wanted to be in a profession where I could fight back, and not in one where I could be fired and have to keep still for the good of the cause."[9]

Losing that first teaching job pushed Mac in several new directions. Eventually, the fundamental unfairness, not to mention the illegality of that situation, would entice Mac into enrolling in law school. In the meantime, however, Mac advanced his education by enrolling at the University of Oklahoma. He very much liked going to Oklahoma's flagship university. "It's better than being at home, looking at a mule in the tail from sunrise 'til sundown."[10] He earned a bachelor's degree from the University of Oklahoma on June 5, 1917, with a "concentration in law preparation."[11]

His short-term plan was to attend law school in Oklahoma or perhaps Texas. But that plan turned out to be short-lived. Two months earlier, President Woodrow Wilson entered the United States in what became World War I. The war had ravaged Europe for the previous two and a half years. Mac and many of his graduating classmates joined the armed forces. He enlisted in the U.S. Navy for a four-year term. At five foot ten inches tall and weighing 145 pounds, he was in excellent health. The war came as a shock—he would soon face his first life-threatening challenge, one that caused him to leave Oklahoma and his family for the first time in his life. He was only twenty-three.

2

Mac Joins the U.S. Navy, 1917

Mac's official enlistment record and everything he did in the U.S. Navy from his date of enlistment, December 11, 1917, to his honorable discharge, January 31, 1919, is set forth in a single-page, military style record.[1] That dry, jargon-laced page reveals only those facts that were important to the navy—naval rating S2c—he spent 330 of the 416 days he was in the navy as a patient in sick bay at the U.S. Naval Hospital in Great Lakes, Illinois—age twenty-three years and three months old on the day of enlistment—blue eyes, brown hair, ruddy complexion—proficiency rating 2.8—sobriety rating 4.0—obedience rating 4.0. At the time, the average rating for U.S. Navy sailors was 3.6. Mac excelled in obedience and sobriety. His low rating in proficiency was understandable. He nearly died. He was not medically qualified for reenlistment, so the navy paid him $14.50, and gave him an honorable discharge from active duty. The facts on his discharge order were accurate, save for his date of birth; the navy said he was born in 1895, but his birth certificate says 1894.

The Naval Station Great Lakes, built exactly as ordered by President Theodore Roosevelt in 1904, was the navy's largest training facility. Located on the southwestern shore of Lake Michigan, it was then and still is the navy's only boot camp. When Mac arrived, he would have seen 39 permanent brick

Mac joins the United States Navy, 1917.

buildings on a 165-acre plot. He joined approximately 1,500 other young sailors in training. At the close of the war, the camp had 776 buildings. About 125,000 sailors had been trained there by the end of the war. Today, approximately 40,000 recruits pass through boot camp there, with an estimated 7,000 recruits on board the installation at any time.

Mac spent 79 percent of his naval service in the hospital. The navy's stark one-page discharge record reveals nothing about why he spent 330 days in sick bay or why he never left his initial basic training base. But his family's records confirm that neither the harsh northern Illinois winter weather nor the U.S. Navy's hospital treatment was good for Mac. Two months into his basic training, Mac contracted pneumonia, and was put in sick bay on March 3, 1918, recorded as "seriously ill." His pneumonia lingered, got better, then relapsed to a second, near fatal stage on March 23, 1918.

Mac wrote a few short letters to his parents during his long hospital stay. The navy communicated with his mother via Western Union. They sent Keziah three telegrams. The March 12, 1918, telegram read, "DESPATCH—UNITED STATES NAVAL HOSPITAL GREAT LAKES—OFFICIAL BUSINESS—GOVERNMENT RATES—APR. 22, 1918—MRS. K. MCFARLAND, ELSBORO OKLA.—MCFARLAND CONDITION IMPROVED. H. E. ODELL."

The next telegram, dated April 27, 1918, read, "DESPATCH—UNITED STATES NAVAL HOSPITAL—OFFICIAL BUSINESS—GOVERNMENT RATES—MRS. K. MCFARLAND, EARLSBORO, OKLA.—MCFARLAND CONDITION NO IMPROVEMENT—H. E. ODELL."

The third and final telegram, dated April 28, 1918 read, "DESPATCH—UNITED STATES NAVAL HOSPITAL, GREAT LAKES—MRS. K. MCFARLAND—MCFARLAND CONDITION SERIOUS, RECOVERY DOUBTFUL."

Little is known today about how much the McFarland family in rural Oklahoma in 1918 knew about the influenza pneumonia pandemic during that year. Even so, it is likely that Mac's diagnosis, the fact that it lingered so long and that he underwent a serious operation, caused great anguish for his parents and siblings. But as was common in the family, they did not dwell on things like that or talk much about it. The 1918 pneumonia pandemic killed many people in the United States and more than twenty-five million people worldwide. It was called the *Spanish Influenza* because a large flu outbreak occurred in Spain in May and June of 1918. However, modern history tells a different story. It appears to have originated in March 1918 among U.S. soldiers in Kansas; about five hundred men there were infected, among whom forty-eight were listed as having died of pneumonia. Whatever its origin, by September 1918, six months after Mac was diagnosed, the influenza had spread to the civilian population of America. It first reached epidemic proportions in Boston, and then spread to New York, Philadelphia, and beyond, following the railroad lines. Twelve thousand people died of the influenza in America in September 1918, but the death toll reached ninety-five thousand in October—the highest death rate for any single month in U.S. history. The published rate was five dead for every one hundred people, or 5 percent of the United States population.[2] Penicillin was not yet invented, and antibacterial treatment was limited.

Mac apparently suffered a collapsed lung, which necessitated a difficult surgery on March 23, 1918. His surgeons elected a rarely used posterior incision—from his back—to remove part of a rib, and vent built-up fluids in his lungs. They called it a "vicarious war wound." He carried the effects of that surgery for the rest of his life. But that was not the worst of it; his postoperation complications included pericarditis, pleurisy, and emphysema. His nurses wrote letters to the family, but the letters mostly caused anxiety rather than reassurance.

When Keziah McFarland got the April 27 telegram reporting Mac's recovery as "doubtful," she must have known the likely outcome—death. She took the train to Great Lakes and stayed at Mac's bedside through the end of May 1918. Finally, Mac stabilized, and his mother went back to Earlsboro.

Mac stayed in the hospital for another six months. His doctors said he was far too ill to be discharged, even on sick leave. He never finished basic training as an enlisted man. Although he was honorably discharged from the hospital and the navy on January 31, 1919, he remained in the U.S. Navy Reserve for decades. His commanding officer, along with the Naval Board of Medical Examiners, recommended "disability in the line of duty," and he took the train home to Earlsboro. While it could not possibly have been imagined by Mac, or the navy, Mac would eventually retire from the navy with the rank of commander.[3]

Over the next sixty-five years, Mac refused to discuss those dark days in the hospital or his near-death experience. He remained dedicated to the U.S. Navy for the rest of his life. It was an experience that would loom large when he reached the U.S. Senate on the eve of World War II. His health and hospital experience accounts for his abrupt decision to leave Oklahoma in early May 1919, and take his chances out west in Arizona. He saw it then as a mostly underpopulated desert on the southwestern frontier, rich with the promise of opportunity and hope. Its reputation for a dry climate that helped men with lung conditions was a key part of his decision. He boarded the Rock Island Line, headed south out of Oklahoma, and connected with the Southern Pacific Line in Texas. In his naval uniform with only ten dollars in his pocket, he arrived in Phoenix, Arizona, and took his enlisted man's naval uniform off for the last time. He said almost nothing in his 1979 autobiography about his hospitalization or his medical condition in 1919, but he did say how wonderful it felt to wear his navy uniform all the way to Arizona. People were wonderful to ex-serviceman, he said.[4]

His immediate family had moved west—from North Carolina to Tennessee to Texas—and finally settled in Oklahoma. But Mac's uncle, Poliet Smith, his mother's brother, had emigrated to Phoenix two years earlier. Poliet assured his sister that he would help Mac get started in Arizona. In time, the rest of the McFarlands would follow Mac's westward move.

3

Mac Moves to Phoenix, 1919

As promised, Poliet met Mac at the train station in Phoenix early on the morning of May 10, 1919. Poliet and his family lived in Peoria—a fifteen-mile drive northwest of town. Over the next few weeks, Mac learned about the history of Phoenix. The city got its name from a man named Lord Darrell Dupa, who settled there with the famous Jack Swilling, a Confederate veteran of the Civil War in 1867. Somehow, Dupa knew the area had been part of the Hohokam settlement. He suggested the name "Phoenix," as it described a city born from the ruins of a former civilization. The next year, Phoenix was officially recognized on the Arizona Territory's records as a town. Tom Barnum was elected the first sheriff of Phoenix. His opponents, John A. Chenowth and Jim Favorite, disliked one another so intensely they fought a duel, in which Chenowth killed Favorite. Chenowth survived the duel but was declared ineligible for election, giving the win to Barnum. By 1875, the town had a telegraph office, sixteen saloons, and four dance halls. The townsite-commissioner form of government needed an overhaul, so that year, an election was held in which three village trustees and several other officials were elected. By 1881, Phoenix's continued growth made the existing village structure with a board of trustees obsolete. The territorial legislature passed the Phoenix Charter Bill, providing for a mayor-council government, which took effect on February 25, 1881, when it was signed by Governor John C. Fremont, officially incorporating Phoenix as a city with an approximate population of 2,500.

The 1920 census was 29,053, the town was now a city, and Mac was not as happy as he thought he'd be. Among the papers eventually archived at the Arizona State Library in Phoenix is a poem Mac wrote titled "Exile." He'd never seen the desert, sagebrush, mesquite, or alkali streams. But he was clearly homesick when he wrote his initial impressions shortly after his arrival in Phoenix.

> I am down in Arizona on its cactus-covered plains away down upon the desert. It is a God-forsaken place where you fight with the odds against you when you've taken your last stand. Where you live out in the open among the sagebrush and mesquite with a rattler as a neighbor, not the friendliest to meet—where you fling yourself on a bunk to rest your weary head and you shake the blooming scorpions from the covers of your bed. Oh, I look out upon the sagebrush as I stretch my yearning hands over the long unbroken reaches of the desert's burning sands to a land where brooks are honest. When your lips are parched and dry—not the canyons clear deceptive streams of tasteless alkali. Oklahoma has no mountains full of wealth, mines and drills, but I'd give this whole damned country for one sight of its rolling hills.

Arizona was then a "baby state," and Mac quickly adapted. In a *Time* magazine 1957 interview, he remembered his first impressions differently. "One thing appealed to me when I first came to Arizona. You could look out and see a country just like nature made it—in which beautiful sunset or sunrise were the rule and not the exception. All blended together for a natural beauty of a country with large vistas."

Mac got a job as a teller with Valley Bank in downtown Phoenix, which didn't last long. He told a coworker he didn't think banking was ever going to be his business: "I belong on the other side of the bank. I don't think I'll ever make it there, so I'm going to Stanford to finish my law." He arrived in Phoenix in May 1919. But by the fall of 1920, he was in Palo Alto, California, living in a dorm at Stanford University and studying law.

4

Mac

Law, Political Science, and Sociology, 1919

By the time he was twenty years old, still in Oklahoma, Mac had immersed himself in an intellectual process that would change him, Arizona, and ultimately the nation. He was twenty-three when he moved to Phoenix. A year later, he was accepted at Stanford University. The Stanford Law Department was founded in 1893 by a New York lawyer named Leland Stanford. In 1908, the department began its transition into an exclusively professional school when Stanford's board of trustees passed a resolution to officially change its name from Law Department to Law School. Eight years later, Frederic Campbell Woodward became the first dean of the law school, and he welcomed Mac to the campus. In 1923, the law school received accreditation from the American Bar Association. In 1924, Stanford's law program required a bachelor's degree for admission.

Mac's disciplined studies of law, political science, and sociology gave him a worldview that few in Arizona would recognize until he was almost forty years old. In the 1920s and '30s, higher education was not something Oklahoma or Arizona farm boys sought. But Mac did. He knew something instinctively that others only got from environments that were well-to-do. In Oklahoma, following his release by the U.S. Navy, Mac knew he had to find a life that would suit his intellect. He wanted more than well-tilled farming fields could offer. Stanford suited his deep appetite for acquired knowledge and his thirst to prepare himself for a fully examined and boldly proclaimed life.

Mac studied intensely through four straight quarter sessions. He augmented his legal studies with courses in political science and theories of property and slavery. He read Plato, Aristotle, Cicero, Thomas Aquinas, Machiavelli, Montesquieu, Locke, and Rousseau.[1] He was not the first young law student to simultaneously take courses in other colleges within a university, but he was one of the most voracious learners of his day.

It's hardly a stretch, given Mac's courses at Stanford and the quotations found in his later writings, to assume that Mac knew what Sir Francis Bacon meant in his *Proposal for Amending the Laws of England* by "Books must follow sciences, and not sciences books." For Mac, Bacon's teachings on empiricism found a willing student. Empiricism is science that is "provable or verifiable by experience, or experiment." Bacon criticized many of his academic peers because he thought they spent too much time studying the past and not searching for new discoveries. For Mac, the world of law, political science, and sociology, as he discovered at Stanford, were the disciplines that he would engage and ultimately master. While known as the father of empiricism, Bacon was not himself an avid experimenter, and spent much of his time and skills as a writer. But Mac, over the ensuing twenty years, would create a legal, political, and social atmosphere in Arizona that would profoundly benefit his state and his country. Mac's inherent self-confidence, coupled with his intensive studies in three different fields, came to embody the notion that, instead of relying on the work of past lawyers, judges, and politicians, he would have confidence in himself, *to wit*, "Books must follow sciences, and not sciences books." He believed Francis Bacon who famously advised politicians to pay attention to scientific discovery, which could increase the power of governments.

The intersection between law, political science, and sociology was well defined by the turn of the nineteenth century in higher education. Sociology is rooted in both politics and the philosophy of history. But the state was more a social than political institution. By the time Mac was elected majority leader in the U.S. Senate in January 1951, America had become more political than social. Law *is* the intersection between sociology and political science.

Sociologists study life as a whole, dissecting facts and laws. Political scientists concern themselves with political life and its consequences. Lawyers rely on both disciplines but focus much more intensely on the grand search for justice, equitable resolution of conflict, and tolerance. Perhaps more tellingly, the study of law, unlike sociology or political science, is basic training for advocacy. One of the many things Mac learned at Stanford was that the study of advocacy is a rigorous examination into the substance of the law, how to state it precisely, and how to use it to achieve fair and clear remedies.

In a 1920 Mother's Day letter, written from his dorm room at Stanford to his mother, Keziah, Mac described life at Stanford. "Today is a wonderful day," he wrote, "and as I look out upon the rising foothills, the red roofs of Stanford and the bay in a distance from my window, I am filled with the splendor of it, all the good and great things our Maker has given us."[2] The next year, 1921, Mac got his first taste of national politics. At twenty-five, Mac attended the first of many Democratic National Conventions—as an usher—in San Francisco. He watched the Democratic Party nominate James Cox in a misguided effort to take on the Republican winner, Warren G. Harding.[3]

While it is very uncommon today, Stanford back then recommended law students to spend at least one quarter out of every four, clerking in a law firm. Mac did his first clerkship in the fall of 1921 with the Phoenix firm of Phillips, Cox & Phillips. John C. Phillips headed the firm, took Mac under his legal and political wing, and became Arizona's governor in 1929. His was Mac's first active political campaign. While such a thing is impossible today, Mac sat for and passed the Arizona Bar Examination a year *before* graduating from law school. Passing the bar did not of itself give one the right to practice law; that required a license. But the bar exam was, for Mac, just another stool to knock down on his way to the intersection between political science and sociology.

For the remainder of 1920 and for a good part of 1921, Mac focused his legal studies at Stanford Law on public utilities and water law—two subjects which would hold him in good stead when he ran for public office. But what made Mac different from his law student classmates was that he also took many political science courses at Stanford. He immersed himself so deeply in those studies that he earned a master of arts degree in political science in addition to his law degree. The bachelor's degree in law was awarded in 1922;

the master of arts degree was awarded in 1924, when the political science faculty accepted his master's thesis.

Mac titled his thesis *The Operation of the Initiative and Referendum in California*. The title and the contents of the long, carefully crafted manuscript reveal just how Mac saw the law as the natural intersection between political science and sociology. Politics often collides head-on with social needs and wishes. What's good for the politician is not always good for the citizen he or she is supposed to be serving. Too often, the professional politician's needs are vested deeply in re-election efforts and partisan grip on legislative power. And almost as often, the citizen's needs are vested deeply in a living wage or some other economic reality that won't advance the politician's need to stay in office. That is precisely where the law comes in—it intersects needs running in both directions and channels them into legal and constitutionally protected avenues.

The Progressive Era reform that led to the adoption of the initiative and referendum in many western states occurred in the late 1800s and early 1900s. South Dakota was first in 1884. Mac recommended nothing less than completely restructuring the California constitution. At the turn of the nineteenth century, in California, new laws were being added via the initiative and referendum process in large numbers. The process had nearly emasculated the power of the California legislature. Although Mac was sympathetic to the idea of direct democracy, his research indicated that, as practiced in California, it could lead to tyranny of the majority with substantial damage to minority rights and a heightened effectiveness of special interest groups. So he recommended that the state adopt a new constitution giving the legislature necessary freedom of action while still maintaining its responsibility to the people.[4]

Mac was in the right place and studying political science at the right time, given the title of his thesis. The initiative and referendum are direct legislative devices instituted in California and nearly two dozen other states as part of the reform program during the early 1900s. These political remedies were often lengthy legislative ballot propositions that were not true initiatives or referenda. It is doubtful that many lawyers in Arizona knew much of anything then about the initiative and referendum process, but Mac did. His thesis proves that. The importance of his thesis and the knowledge that writing it gave him was an edge over most other Arizona lawyers, judges, and aspiring politicians. One shining example is Mac's deep understanding that measures enacted by the initiative had special status and prevailed over conflicting measures enacted by ordinary legislative process. This would later make Mac a standout in legislative circles at the highest levels in America.

5

Mac and Florence, Arizona, 1924

Tracking Mac from birth in Oklahoma through his childhood, teenage, and young adult years and on to his stint in the U.S. Navy in Illinois is very much the story of middle America from the turn of the twentieth century to the end of World War I. His move to Phoenix in May 1919 marked the beginning of his lifelong service to and in Arizona. However, Phoenix did not make Mac who he was. Florence, Arizona, deserves that honor.

Florence was then just a village when he moved there, and not very important to the rest of Arizona. But Mac loved Florence and kept it close to his heart for the rest of his life. Its population peaked at about 1,500 in 1924. Geographically, Florence was the exact halfway point between Phoenix and Tucson. Its history was unique because the first farmers there cultivated land that was first plowed by ancient agrarian civilizations a thousand years earlier. What made it different from the rest of Arizona was the Gila River waters had been tapped by the Hohokam, the Native Americans living in the Gila River Valley when the Spanish invaded in the 1500s, were Florence's first inhabitants. The Hohokam is commonly translated as "those who have vanished." Mac never vanished. After his retirement in January 1971, Mac continued to visit old friends in Florence; his grandchildren lived there, and they got to know Florence through his eyes as they drove him back and forth from Phoenix to Florence.

Arizona's history didn't begin when European pilgrims sailed the Atlantic and landed at Plymouth Rock in 1620; it truly began almost a century before when European horse soldiers rode in. The first documented exploration in 1539 was recorded by Marcos de Niza, and followed the next year when Francisco Vásquez de Coronado crossed the Pima River south of Tucson. Arizona was part of Sonora, Mexico, from 1822, but the settled population was small.

In March 1866, Esteban Ramirez filed the first recorded local homestead claim in Florence. The little town's importance came in part from its relationship to the Apache tribe, who lived in the mountains surrounding the town. The federal government had established numerous forts, agencies, and reservations in central Arizona. The business community in Florence contracted with government agencies to supply hay from local farms, livestock from local ranches, and mining supplies to silver strikes around Florence. All government business had to be conducted in the county seat, and in 1909, the state government moved the territorial prison from Yuma to Florence. Its geography between Phoenix and Tucson, with its steady farming community, made it the logical choice for a big business like a prison.

Florence had been part of Old Mexico until the Gadsden Purchase in 1854. It was the last chunk of the contiguous United States to be added to the main body. The Gadsden Purchase facilitated the transcontinental railroad, but Florence had the Butterfield Overland Stage Line running through it. It was the sixth largest settlement in Arizona in 1924, after Tubac, Tucson, Yuma, Prescott, and Fort Defiance, and half the population was Hispanic. But it eventually lost prominence and centrality when Florence was bypassed by the mainline railroad, and a major highway was built on the far west side of town.

Florence, Casa Grande, and a few other nearby towns were sparsely populated when Mac moved to Pinal County. That's not surprising because Arizona was one of the smallest states. In 1864, Arizona only had a recorded population of six thousand people, "not including Indians." By the turn of the century, Arizona grew to just over one hundred twenty thousand. The central part of Arizona was more populous than its borders. Maricopa County was created in 1871. Pinal County followed four years later. Pinal County's beginning was auspicious—eighty-three citizens, all white, petitioned the territorial legislature to carve out a new county from Pima to the south and Maricopa to the north. The petition presented the "need" for a new county because "of the great distance from, and the unavoidable expense of travel, to and from our respective county seats, and the vexatious delay which must necessarily occur in the transaction of business which we are compelled to transact at those places."[1]

The county seat was aptly described as "the town of Florence near the Gila River." That was no easy task since Globe and Safford had bitterly contested for the new county seat. The new courtroom in the new courthouse was as distinct as the beautiful river flowing by, just north of town. It had the only "prisoner dock" in Arizona—for the exclusive use by the Arizona State Prison. Not far from the new courthouse was the infamous Keety Saloon. It featured Baiydale Bourbon, spittoons, foot rails without bar stools, and "large dishtowels hung on the customer's side of the bar so drinkers could cleanse themselves after each libation."[2]

Arizona's legal community has its historical legs in small towns like Florence. Because it was a boomtown—silver mining—it attracted lawyers, who, at the turn of the century, often moved from one town to another, following the current boom. One historic reference quotes a woman describing her lawyer-husband. "Mrs. Sue Summers described how her husband Harry had originally come to Arizona in 1869 to be a miner, but the Indians 'scared him to Tucson, and the law.' He left Tucson to share in Florence's boom as its first district attorney."[3] Mac replaced Harry Summers as county attorney in 1924. The first judge in Pinal County was J. E. O'Connor in 1912. Mac became the Pinal County judge in 1934. By then, the Keety Saloon was long gone, but there were other, less colorful saloons in town.

The Pinal County Courthouse, built in 1891, is an historic three-story redbrick courthouse at Pinal and Twelfth Street. It was actually Pinal County's second courthouse. Known by almost every Arizona lawyer for more than one hundred years, its signature figure was an ornate clock tower. Sadly, the county ran short of money and never installed the clockworks. The builder painted a clock face on it, the time reading 11:44. A modern courthouse replaced it in 1961, but the clock tower stands today, still at 11:44. Mac built his Florence office across the courthouse square.

In 1922, the Gila River supplied irrigated water to Pinal County farms via the Ashurst-Hayden Dam. The tributary to the Gila River is the Salt River, which, in 1922, had been tapped into by the Salt River Valley Users' Association (SRP). The association provided irrigation and municipal water to Phoenix and Maricopa County. Also during 1922, the San Carlos Dam was built, which later became the Coolidge Dam. That facility and the promise it brought to Florence was the dominating political, financial, and social issue in the 1920s. Everyone fought about whether the water in the Gila River, a tributary of the Colorado River, should be included in Arizona's allocation of the nearly three million acre-feet flowing in the Colorado River. The issue was complicated because there was a flow of 2.2 million acres in the Gila River. This dam marked the first major step in the initiation of the San Carlos Project near Florence.[4]

Mac had worked for Governor Hunt on his first campaign. His reward was an appointment as an assistant attorney general. That required a move from Pinal County back to Phoenix in 1922. Mac's autobiography captures that appointment:

> I was appointed Assistant Attorney General under John W. Murphy, where I worked for two years. I remember the first case I argued in the Arizona Supreme Court. It was a test case on the validity of a proposed bond issue by the Salt River Valley Users Project to build the Mormon Flat Dam. It was what was called a "friendly suit." . . . I got the brief the night before the argument . . . The Chief Justice asked me what the Attorney General was doing in the case. I replied, "We are interested in seeing the bonds offered for sale to the people of Arizona are valid." I thought to myself that if they ask me another question, I should say, "I really know very little about the case, you should ask John L. Gust, attorney for the Water Users Association, who wrote the brief." Luckily, he did not ask another question. I did most of the brief work on criminal cases while in the Attorney General's office, but felt I should get into trial work. So, in 1924, I ran for Pinal County Attorney. The law required the County Attorney to reside in the county seat. I won the election, so I moved to Florence, Arizona and have kept Florence as my legal residence ever since.[5]

Over the next sixteen years, Mac became one of Florence's most visible and active citizens. Mac was always there in an important capacity at every public function. He was a major supporter of the local baseball team, rode his own horse in Florence's famous Florence Junior Parada Parade and Rodeo every summer, and initiated scores of community projects. His biographer, McMillan, said, "Mac saw what was needed and went ahead, often without request, and attended to the matter, always shaking hands, and greeting people in his manner. Making contacts and lending support became his métier and was valuable for future political considerations."[6]

Mac was a member of the Phoenix Central Methodist Church, but there was no Methodist church in Florence. So he joined the First Presbyterian, which had been established in 1888. By then, the Catholic church in Florence was eighteen years old. It ministered mostly to the needs of the Hispanic population while the Presbyterian concentrated on the Anglo population, and to some extent, the Pima tribe.[7]

Mac's role in Gila River water issues crossed many lines over two decades. Long before he went to Washington DC, Mac was deeply involved in the building of the 1922 Ashurst–Hayden Dam. The irony would be clear years later when Mac defeated Ashurst and joined Hayden in Congress. Congress had just appropriated five and a half million dollars to build a new dam farther up the Gila River than the Ashurst–Hayden Dam. Building the dam raised again the larger question of dividing the waters between Native American and white farmers. The First Presbyterian Church monitored the native peoples' water rights, and Mac, as a de facto church member, and as Pinal County attorney, played a major role in negotiating the Gila Decree. The new dam was finished in 1930. Its huge, unusual edifice was dedicated by former President Calvin Coolidge, for whom the dam was later renamed.

Ultimately, this dam and the project behind it brought electricity and employment to a vast area of east-central Arizona. Like the Roosevelt Dam on the Salt River, the Coolidge Dam on the Gila River did much to guarantee adequate water for regional farming.[8] Much of that was due to Mac's influence and tireless work on vital infrastructure projects.

Mac used his job as Pinal County attorney to advance both law and policy in local water development. That's because besides being the county prosecutor, he was also counsel to the San Carlos Irrigation and Drainage District.

It was formed by Florence farmers, like Mac. And it followed the lines of the elaborate irrigation system used by the ancient Hohokam. So for Mac, it was only natural that the bounty of the dammed-up water should apply fairly between Native American and white farmers.

◈

Mac lived in Florence throughout the Great Depression. As it did everywhere in America, the depression jolted Arizona's economy, but little Florence avoided the worst problems. Statewide mining interests lost ground, particularly copper which had fallen from 18 cents to 5.5 cents a pound by 1932. Florence's mining industry died. But by the late 1920s, Florence had already started its move to an agriculture economy. Profits declined in the 1930s, but farmers held on to their lands and supported themselves. Florence acquired ornamental street lighting and a new sewage system, paved the main streets, and improved the courthouse, high school, and local churches. During those depression years after 1929, Mac kept current with litigation involving New Deal programs such as farm relief, rural settlement, irrigation, rural electrification, and the San Carlos Project.

Florence Union High School, ca. 1930.

Mac growing cotton, ca. 1950s.

On vacations and after work, he often took long drives. In the thirties, Mac realized that Europeans knew more about the United States than most Americans knew about Europe. Determined not to be like them, between 1930 and 1940 he had visited all but three of the forty-eight states, as well as sections of Canada and Mexico.

In 1931, Mac returned to his roots by expanding his farming interests. He bought a quarter section of land just east of Florence and planted alfalfa and cotton. He kept some of his acreage for decades, and he moved from the old family home on the Florence highway into a modest frame house he purchased adjacent to his law office located in the center of town. His focus on water law from 1931 to 1940 made him a familiar lawyer all over the state as an expert in water law.[9] Settling into life as a country farmer and lawyer, he expanded his private law practice by becoming the primary lawyer for the San Carlos Irrigation and Drainage District. He used their water on his farms and advised them for many years on how to legally run the district.[10]

6

Mac Becomes a Lawyer, 1921

In his autobiography, Mac first mentions becoming a lawyer while he was a student at Stanford University. He decided, even though he was only a first-year law student in the summer of 1920, to go back to Phoenix and take the Arizona Bar Examination.[1] Stanford was on the quarter system then, and Mac had finished the summer quarter. He thought getting a jump on the bar exam would move him into the lawyer field sooner. He also took the 1920 autumn quarter off to serve as a law clerk in the Phoenix office of Phillips, Cox & Phillips. John C. Phillips was a Maricopa County superior court judge, and would later become governor of Arizona.[2] Mac's early instincts about merging law and politics were off to a fast start in 1920.

By then, the Arizona Bar Association was fourteen years old, having been incorporated in Arizona in 1906.[3] Legal practice from 1906 to 1920 is sparsely covered in Arizona history books, but one noted Arizona lawyer and author described those years as "The Listless Bar."[4] In a meeting held in Phoenix in March 1906 at the U.S. District Court, all members of the newly formed bar association were admitted to practice before the federal court, "as a body." A lawyer named Joe Marrow moved the court to accept all members by vouching for their good moral character. William M. Morrow, of the Ninth Circuit Court of Appeals, came to Phoenix on the train specifically for this momentous occasion. Skeptically, he said, "Arizona would be taking quite a chance" by this mass admission of lawyers, *none* of whom had likely taken a bar examination.[5] It was also the case that many of those admitted that day had never attended law school but instead acquired their legal knowledge and skills while clerking in a law firm.

When Mac came back to Phoenix to take the examination, the Arizona Bar Association still had no permanent office and only transacted business in the offices of various members. One place they apparently met often was the old Phoenix Country Club, where, it was said, "many delightful wines were served." Three years later, after Mac had graduated from Stanford Law, the bar association gathered its members in open session, including Mac, to discuss pending legislation. The bar created a surprisingly active and effective committee of lawyers known as the "Ax Committee." It functioned efficiently in opposing bills to fix compensation of attorneys in suits to collect promissory notes and foreclose mortgages. They also quashed bills to reduce fees paid to executors and their attorneys to an "unreasonably low" figure. Perhaps the high note that year was when the bar proposed a disbarment statute, but it failed to pass in the legislature. The Arizona Bar Association continued to be lackluster. A prominent lawyer of that day, James R. Malott, addressed the association's convention in Globe, Arizona, in 1924. He said the bar was "sluggish," and likened its resolutions to those generated on New Year's Eve—"always made but never kept."[6]

Mac found that it took more than passing the exam to be a good lawyer. There was little legal business for men that young or that shy of law school graduation. So he went down to Casa Grande to "prove up" his land claim. While he was at it, he hung out his shingle there, in addition to his law clerking job in Phoenix. He later said it was a good idea—proving up the land claim—but there wasn't much law business in Casa Grande. "Those were hard times," he said.[7]

His father died in 1919, and the next year his mother, Keziah, moved to Phoenix. She brought Mac's youngest brother, Carl, then only fourteen. By Christmas, Mac's sister, Etta Pearl, and her husband, Melton Lawrence Hammen, also gave up on Oklahoma and moved to Phoenix. They set up a new lumber business just outside Phoenix.[8] The next year, Mac's older brother, Forrest, his wife, and his children also made the move. By the end of 1923, all of the McFarland clan had moved from the Dust Bowl and settled in central Arizona. All told, the count was a dozen; they formed a tightly bound group, all with that pioneering spirit that took them from Tennessee to Texas to Oklahoma and then west to Arizona.[9] Mac, thinking about his 1923 classmates at Stanford, said, "Each of us has a jewel to pick . . . a small percent of us will reach that goal, so do not be disappointed if I am one of those who, in the eyes of the world, fail, but try and be content if each of us do our best."

He continued that uncertain notion in his Mother's Day letter to Keziah in 1920. "So when you are thinking of the possibilities of your children and you happen to think of my possibilities, please do not expect much of me, because I am only one, among many and all cannot succeed in what the world calls success. But you should be content if each of us in our humble way succeeds in doing just a little toward making the world a better world. After all that is real success."[10]

Mac was not yet a real lawyer in 1920 and likely did not attend the 1920 Arizona Bar Association convention. He didn't miss much. A constitution for the bar was apparently passed that year, printed on a three-by-five-inch, seventeen-page paper-bound booklet. It is neither dated nor signed. But James Murphy described the events surrounding its passage in his book, *Laws, Courts, and Lawyers Through the Years in Arizona*. It records election of a president, vice president, secretary, and treasurer and declares all members of the legal profession, "whose names appear on the records of the Supreme Court to be members of the association." Dues were three dollars per year. It had a grievance committee, but no report for activity in 1920.

By 1926, Mac was practicing law full time. That was the year a well-known disciplinary case stirred much discontent in the Arizona bar. It involved an attorney who "allegedly" took money belonging to a client. Initially, the bar did nothing about it. So the Arizona attorney general filed a direct proceeding in the Arizona Supreme Court. The justices at the time were A. G. McAlister, Henry D. Ross, and Alfred C. Lockwood. Mac knew them all. By the time he became a supreme court justice, in 1965, all of them had died. What stirred up the bar association was its initial failure to institute a disciplinary case, forcing Attorney General John Murphy to act.

State law defined unprofessional conduct and a process by which lawyers could be disciplined.[11] The evidence presented to the justices established that the lawyer, Weldon J. Bailey, had collected $190.32 for his client, commingled the money with his own funds, and failed to deposit the money in his client's account. The client said he'd inquired about his money "at least 30 times," but never got his money. Once the case was filed, the bar association investigated and found out that Bailey, in 1914, had been held in contempt of court in Montana for practicing law without a license. In 1915, Bailey, who was licensed to practice in Nevada, was disbarred there. Eventually it was determined that Bailey was disbarred in California and Alabama, but Bailey's multistate bar association problems had little to do with the important legal precedent established in the Bailey case. That single case started a strong movement in Arizona for its bar association to root out unethical lawyers and become a mandatory-membership bar. The Arizona Supreme Court, in disbarring Bailey, established a tradition that is still robust today. The court famously said:

> Learning is not the only qualification of a lawyer. He should be honest, truthful and fair, not only in his dealings with his clients, but with the courts. Indeed, these are the great desiderata in the composition of the true lawyer . . . If it is discovered he is not dealing with his clients honestly it becomes the duty of those who have licensed him to take from him his license, however unpleasant it may be. It is the order of this court that the name of Weldon J. Bailey shall be stricken from the roll of attorneys of this court, and that he be permanently precluded from practicing as such attorney in all the courts of this state.

By this action, the Arizona Supreme Court publically formulated its common-law right to control and discipline attorneys. Prior to this case, the state legislature claimed the right to discipline lawyers under state statute. But the legislature had no machinery to investigate lawyers and no particular interest in inquiring into complaints of malpractice. Prior courts felt hamstrung. The result was that little could be done because any person who was not a member of the bar association could be admitted by the supreme court, sign the roll, pay his dues, take the oath, and disappear from the state, just like Bailey did. The bar's history, as recorded by James M. Murphy, noted that "real estate men, abstractors, and insurance men frequently acted in the capacity of self-appointed lawyers, giving the bar a bad image."[12] In 1933, this reality changed when the Arizona Supreme Court transformed the Arizona Bar Association into a fully integrated bar. Arizona became the tenth state in the union to have an integrated bar. The rule of law had finally come forth to aid those injured by dishonest lawyers.

Mac held a direct connection to these important changes in the bar. He was appointed to the position of assistant attorney general by John W. Murphy, the man who filed the Bailey disbarment case. He held that position for two years, and argued his first case before the Arizona Supreme Court. It turned out to be a test case on the validity of a proposed bond issue by the Salt River Valley Water Users Association. They used the bond proceeds to build the Mormon Flat Dam. Mac called it a "friendly suit."[13]

By the time Mac was elected as an associate justice on the Arizona Supreme Court, and when he served as Arizona's chief justice, Mac ruled on scores of disciplinary cases against lawyers.

7

Mac Runs for Pinal County Attorney, 1924

The Arizona Territory, formed in 1863, died in 1912 when it became a state. Arizona only had four counties in 1863; Pima, Mohave, Yuma, and Yavapai. Two of them, Mohave and Yavapai, were north of the Gila River. They were the "boss" counties in 1863. But Pima County boasted that it was south of the Gila; its county seat, Tucson, had been flexing its statewide muscles for thirteen years. The *Arizona Graphic* told Tucson's story in an 1899 article:

> Its narrow crooked dusty business streets, and one-story mud shops are forbidding, and the visitor must stay long enough to look inside these shops and get acquainted before he approaches the worth of the town... Congress Street, the main business thoroughfare was laid out by cattle going to and from the corrals, in the days of the Indians, and some of the buildings on the street look as if the corrals had been robbed.[1]

That description is entirely consistent with Tucson's Mexican heritage. But Florence was an entirely different matter. Florence was a product of the canal boom in the 1880s, which enabled water from the free-flowing Gila River to be diverted for irrigation. From then up to the 1920s, Florence was a significant agricultural enterprise in Arizona. By 1924, most of its citizens were closely connected to farming and everyone there knew the importance of water.

Thirty-seven years earlier, the territorial legislature had sliced up Maricopa County and Pima County to create Pinal County. It made Florence the county seat. The 1920 census pegs Florence with 1,161 residents. It was Pinal County's largest and most important community. By 2015, Florence had grown to 30,770, and was still the county seat, but remained much smaller than Casa Grande, which had grown to 51,460 by 2015. In 2016, Pinal County was the second-fastest-growing county in the United States.

Mac's 1924 decision to run for Pinal County attorney may have been a surprise to people in Arizona's original five counties, but it was the first step in Mac's determined plan to engage both Stanford degrees—law *and* political science. His short tenure as a rural lawyer was not enough for Mac.

In his historical account of lawyers and judges in early Pinal County, John Murphy said:

> The careers of early Pinal County attorneys can be traced in early court records . . . applicants seeking to practice were rarely denied admission . . . an examining committee administered a series of questions [orally] and reported back with recommendation of admission the same day . . . the wealth of Florence continued to attract attorneys . . . the attorney's wives campaigned to reform efforts by putting up signs, stopping drinking, and establishing a Protestant church.[2]

Mac announced his candidacy for Pinal County Attorney, shortly before he turned thirty. He was single, and deeply involved in Arizona Democratic Party politics and Pinal County civic affairs. Upon his election, he became the youngest county attorney in the state. Because the job required the county attorney to live in the county seat, he moved to Florence. His biographer, McMillan, set the time and place eloquently:

> Florence possessed a unique ambience where the old West retained a living presence even as the town endeavored to embrace a significant modernized future in the state as a potential transportation and trade center. Like so many

pioneer-era villages, Florence was to be largely disappointed in this hope. Juggled by the whims of transportation routes and depletion of mining resources, the town, outstripped by other communities, never realized its dreams. It endured, however, encapsulated in its historical past, and still strong in agriculture and county politics. Mac proved a stalwart townsman of Florence and kept its interests and comforts at heart for the remainder of his life as its most distinguished citizen.[3]

8

Mac and Tommy Fulbright, 1929

Thomas Fulbright was never formal about anything. Just as everybody called Ernest W. McFarland "Mac," they called his longtime law partner "Tommy." The official registration authority for Arizona lawyers is the State Bar of Arizona. Its website, as of 2017, still identifies Tommy. "Educated at Unknown, admitted to practice in 1932, admitted to the State Bar of Arizona May 15, 1926." While the bar may not know Tommy's history or his affiliation with Mac, rural Arizona knew him well. Most Arizona public libraries have a copy of his 1968 book *Cow-Country Counselor*. The bright-orange cover features a white, five-pointed star bordering a short-barreled revolver and a judge's gavel. It beckons readers, "An Arizona attorney's personal, exciting experiences in dealing with rogues and killers."[1]

Tommy's connections to Mac began in 1929 and lasted a lifetime—for both men. Tommy's book includes this note on the back-cover flap: "Tom Fulbright began his career as the first full-time deputy under Ernest W. McFarland, the county attorney of Pinal County who later became United States Senator from Arizona." The book is a delightful mix of anecdotal experience, rural insight, simple law practice, and homespun humor. And as it tells Tommy's story, it speaks volumes about Mac's. They did many of the same things, at the same time, in the same place.

The foreword to Tommy's book sets the stage for how he and Mac practiced law in Florence.[2] "The author, Tommy Fulbright, has been engaged in the practice of law at Florence . . . since 1929. During those years, the community has mushroomed from a village of about fifteen hundred inhabitants to a thriving metropolis of some twenty-five hundred. This rapid growth has not affected Tommy in any way." While no doubt true in Tommy's case, the same cannot be said for Mac.

Florence in 1929, from Tommy's perspective, was composed of "Caucasians, Indians, people of Mexican descent, and a scattering of Negroes among the cotton fields." His law office was a "rather old fashioned place, where in addition to his legal duties, many times he provides luncheon for judges, local and visiting lawyers, and just about anyone who happens to drop in . . . Just off his law library is a small well-furnished apartment, where visiting attorneys, whether 'with or agin' him' are welcome to spend the night during the trial of a lawsuit." Tommy's book, written in 1969, is a first-person narrative gathering in jokes and tales about the times he and Mac had "down in Florence." Mac is prominently introduced in the foreword: "Upon an inner office door appears a sign, 'E. W. McFarland.'" That sets the stage for the rest of the book, which is mostly about Tommy's memories of practicing law with Mac.

Tommy never attended law school, and little is known about his education beyond high school, except that he apparently took a correspondence school course from the LaSalle Extension University in Chicago. That was good enough for Mac. Tommy turned out to be the kind of lawyer Mac needed. His legal knowledge might have been questionable, but Tommy had something else. His longtime friend, Allan Perry, knew what Mac knew: "[Tommy's] knowledge of what makes people tick is virtually limitless." Mac's intellect and Tommy's people skills made for a formidable trial team. They tried every case together and rarely lost.

The first story in Tommy's memoir is called "They Ain't So Damned Smart." He came to Florence from Phoenix in April 1929 as Mac's first full-time deputy county attorney. By then, Mac was completing his third term as Pinal County attorney. Things were slow that first year, but in March 1930 everything changed for the better. The much anticipated dedication of the Coolidge Dam, impounding the waters of the upper Gila River, came to town. It changed farming, which was almost everything, in Pinal County, and Florence. The dedication was attended by those who Tommy called a "host of dignitaries and many others, including Will Rogers and Cal Coolidge." They dammed the Gila to supply irrigation water to "fifty thousand acres of the lands of the peaceful, patient Pimas, and Papagos, who for centuries had dealt with the desert sands with but primitive means of cultivation and meager sources of water. It was also intended to irrigate fifty thousand acres of white lands of those who for decades had toiled, pioneered and waited for water in the Casa Grande Valley."

Florence had a chamber of commerce by then. Tommy said, "Most business and professional men and all others 'of any consequence' belonged. Now that they had water for farming, all they needed were two more things. A new hotel and a good baseball team. A baseball team was acquired by the simple expedient of importing proficient players and placing them on the town's payroll at dummy jobs, with the taxpayers footing the bill. Nobody complained."

The only hotel in town was the one Tommy was living in a year after Mac hired him, the Florence Hotel. It was a rambling two-story adobe, owned by Joe Spires, a local character. Tommy described Spires: "He was elderly, a barrel of a man, habitually had a cigar in his mouth, was cockeyed, and could only walk with his heavy cane. His only source of income other than his hotel was his poker playing, in which he had no peers in Florence, which never has been noted for its easy marks in this game of skill."

Joe Spires, never a happy man, was particularly upset about the chamber of commerce plan to build another hotel. "Are you sure they will do it?" Joe asked. "They will," his fellow poker players said. Tommy and Mac were influential members of the Florence Chamber of Commerce. Spires knew that. Either Tommy or Mac told Spires, "We just found a place to build the hotel about three blocks south from here. We're all behind it, and it will go. And there is a bunch of mighty smart men involved." Joe, slightly cockeyed, said in his drawl, "Well, they ain't so dammed smart, or they wouldn't be here in Florence. I wouldn't be here myself if I could sell out."[3]

An out-of-town guest at the Florence Hotel came downstairs early one morning and remarked to Joe, "You have a mighty nice little town here." Joe snarled back, "Yes, we do have a nice little town, and it would be a good town except for all the sons-o'-bitches who live in it."

In 1930, Mac was defeated when he ran for another term as Pinal County attorney. It was not unusual for county attorney positions to go back and forth in rural Arizona. And, as was the custom of the times in rural Arizona, he and Tommy continued to practice private law, out of the same little office described in Tommy's book.

In the chapter titled "The Helpful Defendant," Tommy describes how he and Mac practiced law in the thirties. "The first inquiry of a client," Tommy recalled, "is what's this going to cost? This is especially true if the client intends to pay. If he has ideas of not paying, or of putting up a small retainer—as little as he can get by with—he exhibits but little concern about the fee. And this is the first tip-off, particularly in criminal cases, for the lawyer to look at his hole card.

"Most clients," Tommy continued, "are curious about how the fee is set." Tommy's answer was, "It all depends on whether I furnish the evidence, or you furnish the evidence." Mac and Tommy were confronted with that very situation in the defense of a man named Billy. He was charged with grand larceny. Billy was part of a "closely knit group of nesters on the desert west of Casa Grande who lived without the law." As Tommy remembered it, "this was our first case against the county attorney's office after we had been involuntarily retired from office."

Billy was accused of stealing some steers, but Tommy said it was "a weak case as cow cases always were. The cow's owners tracked them to close to Billy's camp on the desert, but he denied all knowledge of 'em. There were suspicious fragments of evidence, but they were circumstantial. Early on a Saturday morning, Billy and a carload of his buddies came to see us. He said he and his friends, including Bob McClain, who was the stud monkey of the outfit because of his brushes with the law, had a good idea as to how his case should be handled."

Bob told Tommy and Mac, "We've been talking about the case and this is what we think we ought to say. We could have had a dance out in the desert the night Billy stole them steers, with nineteen or twenty of us there, and then we could all swear that Billy was with us. What do you fellers think of that?"

Tommy recalled this situation as "unusual, to say the least. Mac hummed and stuttered for a minute. Then in his inimitable Will Rogers Okie drawl,

Mac said, 'Now Bob, we can't do that. It is not the way Tommy and I do things.'"

"Why can't we?" said Bob. "Have you boys got something better?"

Mac told them, "Yes. They don't have much on Billy, and those fellows in the county attorney's office are not fools. Let's let it drag along, and they may never bring it to trial. If they do, I think we can beat it."

Billy, Bob, and their friends left. Mac and Tommy talked about it. They could tell Billy was not convinced and was greatly puzzled as to why they had discarded an iron-clad alibi. In time, the case died a natural death, "as cow cases often do."

Tommy gave his readers a good look at homesteading in Pinal County. "It was all about following World War I. A large area of the desert, south and west of Casa Grande, was opened to homesteaders. Mac was one of them. The opportunity to acquire lands followed the usual government pattern. Home seekers and immigrants from all over came to file entries, occupy their selections, and make the required improvements for issuing patents. The improvements included a dwelling, a privy, fencing, and in all instances, a well and a windmill. They could prove up on a section of land. Mac did. His section was one of many dotted with the roosting places of nesters. But Mac was no nester; he had a place in town. A man Tommy called Slim did not. Slim eked out an existence in various and sundry ways, most of which were outside the law," Tommy recalled. These men and their families attracted others to Pinal County. They had "similar habits and philosophies, who in brief were one for all, and all for one. They made their own laws and lived by their own code, and so constituted a serious and ever present problem for law enforcement agencies of Casa Grande. Convictions were all but impossible. This was the set up when I came to Florence in 1929."

Slim was charged with grand larceny for stealing a windmill. Slim, Tommy said, "was a short, slight, stooped tubercular. He intimately knew the whole desert and all the goings on. On a cold wintery day morning, Slim came to our office in his old Model T, and after warming his hands on our stove, he gave us a rundown on his problem. We asked if he could make bond and he said yes." That was not as improbable as it might sound. Slim was a good well-driller and drilled wells at a low figure, as "he always furnished second hand casing the ownership of which no one inquired about." Slim said Rye

Mills, the deputy sheriff at Casa Grande, was "hot on his trail. We gave him a bail bond form and told him to get people to sign it.

"A few hours later, Rye Mills showed up in our office, and asked if we'd seen Slim. We asked why he wanted to know. He said he had a warrant on Slim and had been looking for him for two days. We told him Slim was our client and we would surrender him within forty-eight hours. We did. The windmill had been dismantled and was in Slim's possession. He'd been caught red-handed. But Slim had a story to tell, and he told it well. The jury bought it and ruled in his favor. We had our doubts about the story, but never asked Slim if it was true. It was his story, and the jury liked it."

Mac and Tommy tried another case involving a man named Clabber Warner in the early thirties. In the eastern part of Pinal County, there was a road leading from the highway between Mammoth and Winkleman. The road petered out twenty miles east, at the opening of the Aravaipa Canyon. Twenty people lived in that rugged rocky canyon. All of them raised Angora goats for their unexcelled white wool. Two of the toughest characters in the Aravaipa were Sam Baker and Clabber Warner. No one knew what Clabber's real first name was. Everyone knew he was called Clabber because of the "huge proportions of his hind end, which appeared to have the consistency and movability of clabber milk. He was about as big in circumference as he was in height."

Sam and Clabber were not friends. Clabber had threatened to kill Sam with the single-action Colt .45 revolver he always stuck in his belt. When Sam went to town shopping in Mammoth, he had to cross right by Clabber's homestead. Sam knew about Clabber's Colt, so he always carried a double-barreled shotgun loaded with a bird shot, used to shoot birds on the wing.

One day, Sam and his mother were going to Mammoth in their Ford Model T. Clabber was on his front porch as usual, but seeing Sam, he ran out to the road with his .45 drawn. "Sam stopped and aimed his shotgun at Clabber. That persuaded Clabber to stop, turn around and waddle at his fastest pace back to his house. Sam peppered Clabber in his rear end, which offered a broad target." Clabber was not seriously hurt but was deeply offended. He insisted on charges against Sam.

Tommy and Mac were retained to defend Sam. They tried the case in the old Pinal Courthouse in 1934. Everyone from Aravaipa was present, along with half the people in Florence. The county attorney put Clabber on the stand and walked him through the story about Sam peppering him with buckshot as he tried to run back to his house. Mac handled Clabber's cross-examination.

Mac's first question was, "Why do they call you Clabber?"

Clabber was embarrassed and answered, "I don't know."

Mac persisted, "Isn't it a fact that you are commonly known up and down the Aravaipa Canyon as Clabber Warner because of your big hind end?"

Clabber finally and reluctantly said, "Yes."

Tommy remembered the case as won at that point because the jury and everybody in the courtroom laughed. "When a jury laughs with you and not at you, you immediately know they are on your side. Mac then called Sam and his mother who told the jury about the threats Clabber had made to kill Sam. The jury quickly found Sam not guilty." And, Tommy said, "It took two weeks and several trips to Florence for the old pioneer Dr. Huffman to get all the bird shot out of Clabber's anatomy."

Unquestionably, the most dramatic and violent case Mac and Tommy prosecuted in Florence was a case Tommy described as the "Unholy Three." They were, he said, a "congenial, convivial group, born, spawned in hell, and sired by the devil. They were as deadly as a nest of psychotic sidewinders." He was talking about Irene Schroeder, Glenn Dague, and Vernon Ackerman. The case against Schroeder and Dague ultimately ended in his death by electric chair in the Rockview Prison in Pennsylvania on February 23, 1931. The three killed a Pennsylvania highway patrolman, Corporal Brady Paul, but they were able to escape from police among a hail of bullets. Following that murder, on December 27, 1929, Schroeder, Dague, and Ackerman, "blazed a trail of murder, robbery, and violence across at least a dozen states that ended in their capture in the rugged Estrella Mountains a few miles south of Phoenix."

Mac and Tommy prosecuted criminal charges against "The Unholy Three." They also participated in the armed manhunt for them in Florence on January 13, 1930.

About three o'clock that day, the Unholy Three arrived in Florence. Their finances were running low and they knew they were being chased and watched in every town in America. At the high school on South Main Street,

Ackerman and Dague got out of the car. Irene Schroeder drove slowly north toward the Standard gas station. Ackerman and Dague followed on foot, but on opposite sides of Main Street. They figured "a lone woman might be able to beg some help at the gas station and thus obviate the need for another holdup." About the time she was trying to get free gas, Deputy Sheriff Joe Chapman stopped at the station. The owners, Steve and Harris Branaman, told Chapman she'd asked for help, but they turned her down.

"We figured a woman who is driving a late-model Chrysler should have enough money to buy gas."

Deputy Chapman walked over to the car and asked for her driver's license and registration. "Suddenly, he remembered a wanted poster for Glenn Dague and Irene Schroeder and immediately recognized her." She had been dubbed in the newspapers as the Tiger Woman. Chapman took no chances and said, "Put your hands up." But Irene slumped over on the steering wheel and sounded the horn. Ackerman crossed the street and stuck his gun in Chapman's back.

"It was a dramatic standoff: Joe had the blonde covered, and the ex-con had his gun in Joe's back. Suddenly Dague appeared, knocked the gun out of Joe's hand and said to Irene, 'go into that service station and pull those damn telephone wires loose.' Irene leaped into the rumble seat and Ackerman ordered Chapman into the front seat, between him and Dague who was under the wheel. They drove fast on Main Street, past the bank, and past Sheriff Laveen and Constable Whitlow on the curb. Nobody noticed."

The story from there was widely covered in the news. They robbed Deputy Chapman, used his money to buy oil, gas, and food. They went north to Picacho Lake where the road ended. They huddled and then told Chapman they would kill him first if any officers showed up. From there, they drove to Chandler, just south of Phoenix. The officers in Chandler included Lee Wright, an old-time police officer, tall and rangy, with a heavy drooping mustache and a black cowboy hat. With him was another officer, Lee Butterfield. Both were armed with .45 caliber pistols and shotguns. They'd been told to be on the lookout for a 1929 Chrysler coupe coming from the south. Dague must have seen the officers waiting because he turned the car on two wheels and tried to race out. Inside the car, Chapman tried to wrestle a gun away from Irene. The Chandler officers opened fire, and Dague and

Ackerman fired back. The gunfight only lasted a few seconds. Wright was killed, and Butterfield was badly injured. They were out in the open. Deputy Chapman was in the heavy car, but still lost three fingers on his hand and had buckshot in his ear. None of his captors were hit. Dague turned the car around and head north. A short time later, they turned west into the Estrella Mountains a few miles from Phoenix. Within a few miles, the car died, and they abandoned it.

What was not reported was the fact that both Mac and Tommy were in the posse, carrying guns, like many other Florence citizens. Like any other small town, the kidnapping of Deputy Chapman off Main Street spread like wildfire. Within a short time, almost every adult male was armed and was in some kind of vehicle trying to find the kidnappers. They knew one officer had been killed in Chandler, and two others were wounded. Mac and Tommy rode with Ace Gardner and Elmer Coker. Tommy had an old .25-25 rifle. Mac was armed, but Tommy forgot the caliber of Mac's gun by the time he wrote his book in 1969. Their car went north across the Gila River, discovered the Chrysler's track, and followed it from there to the Gila crossing. During the night, they joined dozens of other cars and trucks.

Several trackers, led by Chief Sun Dust, followed the trail into the Estrella Mountains. The kidnappers were surrounded, and a short gun battle ensued. It's not known whether Tommy and Mac fired, but they were there. Tommy said, "You could hear the rifle fire ricocheting as they hit the rocks around the kidnappers. Laveen and I had a hell of a time trying to prevent McGee from killing all three. I have thought many times that it might have been just as well had he killed them."

Dague and Irene, nicknamed "the Tiger Woman" by the press, were extradited and later electrocuted in Pennsylvania. Maricopa County tried Ackerman first, but Mac and Tommy filed a kidnapping charge in Pinal County, "just in case." Ackerman was charged with felony murder in Phoenix, but the jury acquitted him. Mac and Tommy went forward with their kidnapping charge in Florence. Ackerman plead guilty, was sentenced to life in prison, and died there, in the prison just a mile from Mac and Tommy's law office.

9

Mac and the Eva Dugan Case, 1930

To say that Mac's life as a prosecutor in the 1920s was unique is a gross understatement. His stint as Pinal County's chief prosecutor was unlike any other prosecutorial office in Arizona for many reasons, but especially because he prosecuted Eva Dugan. Her case invokes what Sir Giles Rooke, a famous Scottish jurist, said in 1797, "Those who make the attack ought to be very well prepared to support it."[1]

Eva Dugan was the first woman to be executed in Arizona and the last person hanged in Arizona. While her execution made her nationally famous, it was the sheer act of disappearing that made her fascinating. Paul Allen, a reporter for the *Tucson Citizen*, said it best: "She had a disappearing act to rival David Copperfield, except that most of those Dugan made disappear didn't come back."[2] Eva had been married five times. Four husbands mysteriously disappeared; she said they were dead. She divorced one husband. Eva was forty-nine at the time of her trial in Arizona in 1927, had a daughter in New York and a father in California, but neither had seen or heard from her in years. She disappeared from them much like she disappeared from Arizona, and eerily like her Arizona employer, a chicken rancher named Andrew J. Mathis, disappeared.

Born in 1878, Eva traveled widely and worked many jobs, including as a cabaret singer in Juneau, Alaska, after making the trek north during the Klondike Gold Rush. Mac described her as "a large, unattractive woman hardened by years of servile work, bitter, angry, and violent." One preprison photograph depicts her as grandmotherly, well dressed with a stylish hat festooned with what appears to be fake jewels. She wears a narrow strand of pearls and has a purse attached to her left arm. Standing beside her is a large, imposing man—he was Sheriff Jim McDonald, the man who led the investigation into her case and who ultimately arrested her. The photo appears to have been taken outside the courthouse just before her trial. Her Wikipedia page features a photograph of the elegant courthouse at 135 Pinal Street in Florence and a photo of the noose they used at her execution on February 31, 1930.

Mathis's chicken ranch was on Oracle Road, four miles north of Tucson. At sixty-three, he lived alone, was in fairly good health, and in need of a housekeeper. He was a bit hard of hearing, and used an ear trumpet. On December 11, 1926, quite by accident, he met Eva Dugan in Tucson. She told him she needed a job. He told her he had one for her—keeping house on his ranch. He hired her that day. She got in his Dodge automobile, and they drove to the ranch. A month later, on January 13, 1927, while Eva was in Tucson, a young boy of about nineteen or twenty years named Jack "bummed her for his breakfast at a Tucson restaurant."[3] He came back to the ranch with her. The next day, January 14, Mathis made a trip into town; he never returned. His neighbors never saw him again.

Eva told the neighbors that Mathis had gone to California by train to borrow money to pay the mortgage on his ranch. She said he'd authorized her to stay at the house, sell his Dodge coupe, and his chickens. On January 15, 1927, Jack drove Eva to Nogales, Arizona, "just for the day." Jack could drive; Eva could not. Eva also told the neighbors that when Mathis returned from California, "they intended to marry." The neighbors could not recall Jack talking. Jack and Eva drove to Bisbee, Arizona, where they stayed at Sander's auto camp. Eva registered under the name B. B. Jones. The camp attendant asked the number in party; Eva said just herself and her husband, Jack. A few days later, they sold Mathis's Dodge in Amarillo, Texas, for six hundred dollars; Eva executed a bill of sale in the name of A. J. Mathis, and took a check made out to Eva Mathis. From there, Eva and Jack went to Kansas City, where Jack disappeared. Eva continued on to White Plains, New York.

Eva was arrested in White Plains, extradited to Arizona, and charged with stealing the Dodge coupe. She apparently put up no defense to the auto theft charge, was found guilty of grand larceny, and sentenced to a relatively short term in jail in Tucson. Nine months later, a man known as J. F. Nash discovered signs of a grave just off the Mathis property line. The Pima County Sheriff's office dug up Mathis's decomposing remains. He had a fractured skull. Eva was charged with his murder, and testified in her own defense. She told the jury that Jack had killed Mr. Mathis by accident, that the men had gone out after supper on January 14 to catch chickens and milk the cow. When they didn't come back, she went looking for them. She saw Jack running, "as though to leave the place, but he got caught in a wire fence." Then, Jack told her what happened.

The old man had wanted Jack to milk the cow, but Jack didn't know how to milk a cow. So, "the old man popped him on the side of the head and asked, 'What in the hell are you good for?'" Then the old man slapped him. So Jack "just throwed [sic] his arm there like that carelessly—didn't think it was such a blow—and caught him right there [indicating] and he fell backwards. He was weak and sick in the stomach anyway, and just a blow like that, unexpected to him, would knock him over and he fell. What wind was left in him I guess went out the rest when he fell. It was hard there. There was nothing at all, but just pure hard ground. Jack tried to resuscitate him but could not; we put him in the auto about 11 o'clock that evening, and Jack took him away. I stayed home. About 5 o'clock the next morning he returned. We agreed to concoct the story of Mathis' going to California *et cettera*."

Eva Dugan's murder trial was sensational, but it was her execution made her nationally famous. Judge Gerald Jones, of Pima County Superior Court, presided over her first and second trials. The Pima County attorney, Claude Smith, prosecuted her. Stanley Samuelson and Otto Myrland defended her at trial, and on appeal. On appeal to the Arizona Supreme Court, the court noted that besides Eva's dubious testimony, the prosecution proved that

Mathis's house had been stripped of practically everything. His ear trumpet was found charred and burned in the stove.

The Arizona Supreme Court said Eva had been proved to be "immoral, profane, and intemperate."[4] While the evidence against her was circumstantial, the court found it sufficiently compatible to support the jury's unanimous verdict. Following trial, the judge sentenced her to death.

Pending appeal, Eva was imprisoned at the state prison in Florence. There is some confirmatory evidence that her supporters, who were against the death penalty, worked hard to get Governor John Calhoun Phillips to commute her sentence. He was the same John C. Phillips who gave Mac his first law job—clerking in his Phoenix firm in 1921. Two reports confirm Eva giving interviews from prison at one dollar per interview. While awaiting her appeal, she "made her own burial dress, a beaded, silk jazz dress. She bought her own coffin by selling embroidered handkerchiefs she made in her cell. The day before her hanging, the guards heard a rumor she'd cheat the gallows by suicide. They searched her cell and found a bottle of ammonia in her bunk and three razor blades under the collar of her burial dress."

Once the supreme court upheld the verdict and sentence, her only chance of avoiding the death penalty was to declare insanity, and inability to mentally understand the judgment. The prison warden certified in writing he believed her to be insane. Accordingly, the law required a sanity trial on the eve of her execution. Mac's responsibility as Pinal County attorney was to uphold her sanity so her sentence could be carried out.

In his 1979 autobiography, Mac reminisced about Dugan:

> A County Attorney is called on to prosecute all kinds of cases, but the one that bothered me the most was the case of Eva Dugan, who had been convicted of murder in Pima County, and was sentenced to be hanged. The Warden of the prison made a certification that, in his judgment, she was insane, which under the law at that time required that she be tried by a jury to determine whether she was legally sane. It was the duty of the county attorney to uphold her sanity. The case resulted in the jury's finding that she was legally sane. These cases were always tried just before the date of the execution of the death sentence.[5]

The sanity trial was not Mac's first interaction with Eva Dugan. Sometime before her sanity trial, Scott White, the prison warden, called him to discuss a "personnel problem." At about one o'clock in the morning, the warden told Mac they'd just "caught one of the guards in the cell with Eva Dugan. Billie Delbridge wants to put him in jail. What should we do?" Delbridge, who had been secretary to Governor Hunt, was then secretary of the prison. Mac's advice, while legally suspect, reflected the succinct way he solved phone calls in the wee hours of the morning.

"Scott," he said, "You don't want headlines charging one of your guards with having intercourse with Eva Dugan, do you? I would go back there, and fire the guard immediately, then forget about it."

The prison warden did just that. The only record of this nighttime visit between a guard and Eva is Mac's autobiography.[6]

At the sanity trial, Mac demolished Eva's position by inducing the defendant's expert medical witness to anger during intense cross-examination, and then insisting successfully that this temperamental display did not demonstrate insanity. The jury concurred, and on the third ballot voted that Dugan was sane. She was executed the next day, February 21, 1930. Mac did not go to the prison to witness her execution, but both the sanity trial and her grisly execution greatly affected him.

Early that Friday morning, a man called "Daddy Allen" led Eva up the steps to the 1910 gallows platform. She asked him not to "hold my arms so tight, the people will think I'm afraid." Witnesses recalled she swayed slightly and reacted to the bright lighting. The condemned prisoner was tied to a custom-made hanging board. It supposedly prevented the condemned from "slumping."

A guard slowly inched her, while strapped to the hanging board, toward the trapdoor in the middle of the platform, and the hanging noose. Once the noose was tightened around her neck, the warden asked for her final words. She declined. The crowd tensed below as she centered herself on the platform. Then, when the trapdoor sprung down, and her body dropped through, instead of the hard stop followed by a light bounce back upward, her head was completely ripped off her body. It flopped loudly to the ground below, but her head bounced and then rolled to a corner of the platform, almost to the feet of the dumbstruck crowd of gawking onlookers. Two men and three women standing in front fainted. The rest reeled backward, the women scrambling and the men gritting their teeth.

The prison was equipped with a death chamber located one floor above the cells on death row. It had been constructed in 1910 with a scaffold through which the body of the hanged fell into the room below, where witnesses waited to confirm the execution. The first prisoner executed there was Jose Lopez on January 5, 1910. Eight more men went through the trapdoor between 1910 and 1930. Eva was the first and only woman to be executed by hanging. And she was the first and only prisoner to suffer "execution-malfunction." The cause was ultimately determined to be a gross miscalculation of the length of the drop. The drop length through the trapdoor is regulated by the slack in the hangman's rope. The slack is largely based on the prisoner's weight. The evaluation, in part, came from witness reports of her body "plunging," her neck "snapping," and her body "rolling." The rope, scores of pictures, and the actual hanging board are on display at the Pinal County Historical Museum in Florence. The display at the museum wryly notes the official summary. "There was a miscalculation when Eva Dugan was hanged on the morning of February 21, 1930. Her head was jerked off. Hanging then went out of fashion."

She was fifty-two years old. There is no record of how or even whether someone reattached her head to her body before she was buried. Eva Dugan's decapitation horrified Arizona and a good part of the rest of the nation. By 1934, Arizona abandoned the gallows for the gas chamber.

Mac wrote, "I could imagine her hanging by the rope. But this she never did, because they gave her too much rope. As a result, she was decapitated. Her head went one way and her body went another. The sight was so gruesome to those who saw it that the law was changed to the use of gas rather than death by hanging."[7]

Eva Dugan's sanity trial was not Mac's last bat at saving someone from or sending someone to the death chamber at the Arizona state prison. But Dugan's execution helped Mac make a large decision to change the direction of his career. "I became tired of pushing people into the penitentiary." So, he ran for election to the Pinal County superior court judgeship in the upcoming 1930 elections.

10

Mac, Clare, and Their Children, 1925 to 1929

Clare Collins Smith was beautiful, talented, and devoted to Mac. They met during the Christmas holidays in 1919 at Stanford. Mac was in law school, and Clare was an undergraduate studying music. Mac's biographer, McMillan, said, "She was an exceptional person by all accounts. From Illinois, she matriculated at Stanford in the fall of 1919 for studies in music, concentrating on voice. She was proficient enough to be considered an opera candidate, but her musical hopes were crushed by a developing throat condition. So she moved to the drier climate of Arizona and finished college at Arizona Teachers College in Flagstaff. She moved to Florence in the 1920s with her mother, Ann Collins Smith. When she and Mac married in 1925, she quit teaching and commenced her role as wife and manager of the McFarland house on the old highway."[1]

They had four happy years, but things changed in 1929. It was a bad year for the entire country, not just rural Arizona: The South was awash in strife, death, and dislocation. Jim Crow ruled. Southern textile manufacturers used only nonunion labor. Northern textile manufacturers went south to take advantage of special taxes, abundant water supply, and lenient labor laws. A seventy-two-hour workweek was par. The Valentine's Day Massacre in Chicago was on everyone's front page when fourteen members of Bugs Moran's gang were mowed down by Al Capone. Sixty percent of American households lived on less than two thousand dollars per year. A new president, Herbert Hoover, came into office in March. The stock market crashed in October. The year that had looked so prosperous in January for businesses and farmers looked bleak in October.

Their firstborn son, William Ernest McFarland II, born in 1927, was just two years old in 1929. In mid-February of that year, Jean Clare, their second child, was born at the same hospital as her brother, but she died there when she was just three days old. Mac and Clare went into seclusion and coped as best they could. They had wide family support and the heartfelt sympathy of all of Florence and a large part of Pinal County. While healthy babies were common, so was infant death all over America. Families tried to accept it and conceived again. But the death of Jean Clare was not the McFarlands' only loss; two days later, they lost William Ernest.

The *Arizona-Blade Tribune*'s February 15, 1929, issue commiserated for all of Florence. "It was the second loss by death to visit their home within a few days. Their oldest child, a son, was stricken with a serious infantile disease and passed away after only a short illness."

Even without the benefit of a written record, it is safe to assume, from all that is known about the strength of character of both Mac and Clare, they grieved in private. The people of Florence gave them time to heal. Mac and Clare faced the dreadful reality of losing both children in such a short time and at such a tender age. For Clare, all efforts to keep building a happy and welcoming home stopped. For Mac, all efforts to advance his law practice and lend help to every community project that came along was put off. Tommy Fulbright ran the law practice, and Clare's mother looked after the McFarland house. They quit socializing, and Mac spent more time in local bars. But five months later, Mac decided they both needed to get out of Florence for the summer, and the couple took an extended trip.

Mac wrote almost nothing in his autobiography about losing William Ernest and Jean Clare. Perhaps to thwart the memory of that painful time, his only reference in 1979 was painfully oblique. Mac wrote six sentences; only one of them mentioned the death of his children. And even that one connected their deaths to his term as county attorney:

It was in the middle of my term as County Attorney that Clare and I lost our children. I thought it would be good for us to get away for a while on a trip. We still didn't have any money, but my brother-in-law, L. M. Harman, had begun to succeed in the lumber business. I had invested a little money in his business, so he helped us make our trip. We went on a boat through the Panama Canal, up to New York, then over to England, Scotland, Ireland, France, Belgium, and Germany, and back. Clare and I went to Los Angeles to board the old S.S. Mongolia. This cost us $125 each for the sixteen days it took to go from Los Angeles via the Canal to New York.

Other than the small news item in that Florence newspaper, little was said publically regarding the loss of their children. But there is a large record of the trip they both hoped would give them the strength to go on. They traveled by train from Florence to Los Angeles, where they boarded a cruise ship that took them, via the Panama Canal, to New York. The trip, Mac said "was to help Clare with her physical and mental condition after the death of our children. Those deaths broke her heart and she never fully recovered."

Mac's recollection of the trip in 1979 included small details as well as a large overview of international travel. He described the first ship they took from Los Angeles to the Panama Canal. "It was a steam turbine-driven twin-screw passenger-and-cargo ocean liner launched in 1922 for the Peninsular and Oriental Steam Navigation Company (P&O). She originally sailed from the United Kingdom to Australia. Later in P&O service, she often sailed the Panama Canal. By 1929, when Clare and I boarded her, she had been converted to oil fuel."

Eventually that old ship was sold to a New Zealand company and renamed the SS *Rimutaka* in 1939. Mac recalled it was "ill fitted with small stuffy rooms." In letters back to his family in Arizona, Mac reported that much of his time was spent on deck where he expressed near childlike glee over the new maritime environment of "large turtles, flying fish, porpoises, sharks, and whales." They sailed from Los Angeles to New York City in sixteen days via Balboa, Panama, and Havana, Cuba. Mac smoked Cuban cigars. Clare was silent. She suffered, he said, from "smothering and nerves."

Once they docked in New York, Mac and Clare went about the business of getting ready for Europe. Mac had tried to send a letter home from New

York, but it went astray. In a letter to "Mama and all," dated July 28, 1929, Mac explained:

> I will try and write a few lines this A.M. as today is Sunday and one's thoughts just naturally turn to homeward on Sunday. I wrote you a letter Tuesday night in New York but lost it before I got it mailed. We arrived in New York, by eastern time, about 4 P.M. on the 23rd, took a taxi for the American Express Office, but due to the day-light saving time, which is one hour earlier, we did not get there by 5 P.M. So we took a taxi back to a hotel, which cost us in all $3.80. You see, the office we had our mail and passport sent to was 65 Broadway, which is downtown. There are no hotels close. So we had to go way back to 23rd street to get a reasonable price hotel. I think he just jipped us at that. But of course, we had no way of telling, and were tired, and wore out. Our boat sailed at 11 A.M. The Express Office opened at 9 A.M. We had to get our passport visa, but the British office did not open until 9:30. Our boat sailed from Hoboken N.J., which as you know is across the river in New Jersey. To make it back to 65 Broadway to get our passport visa and make the boat was quite a job. Our taxi driver wanted to rush us there and take us across river for $10. We had enough of him, so told him we would make other arrangements. Wed A.M. we got up at 7 A.M., ate breakfast, took the subway at 23rd and 7th Avenue, which was about two blocks from our hotel. You have to take a train there to 14th Street. The local goes fast. You step right off onto an Express, which takes you like a bullet to the downtown section. We got off at Wall Street, walked about 3 blocks to Am Express. In the mean time we had learned our boat sailed by Eastern time which was 12 noon, daylight savings time. This gave us an extra hour. We got our mail, a letter from Dwight, Carl, and Etta and passport. An American Express man went with us—we got our passport visa and started back at 10 A.M. We went back to hotel the same way, got our grips, and took a taxi to the ferry. It cost 8 cents to board. We got to boat one hour before it sailed at a cost of 78 cents. Now, you are wondering why we did not do this at first. You take these grips plus a package, but you cannot go in a crowd on the subway in the crowded time of day. Then, we did not realize it would be so far back to a hotel. There was a man at the Express office Tuesday eve, but no mail for us. Now we are on board the George Washington. Such a contrast to the Magnolia. You could not find a dining room in Phoenix as swell

as the tourist dining room. Tables for 4, clean linen each meal, large mirrors in center. Everything clean. In fact, the whole of our quarters are nicer than the Adams Hotel. I would say about like the San Carlos. Our cabin has two beds, one bunk, but with good springs, and a davenport on one side, with a nice couch to lounge on. Of course, our room can hardly be as nice as a new hotel, but it is certainly clean and nice, really. It would do credit to any home, small wardrobe, carpet and water basin, medicine cabinet, with large glass. The lounge and reading room is equal to the parlor in a nice hotel. It has large easy chairs, and other works. We were delighted with quarters and meals. Oh boy, what a contrast to the Magnolia. Believe me, I sure eat. Have not missed a meal and retained all of them. The Atlantic is rougher than the Pacific, but they say unusually smooth this trip. Quite a number were sick first two days. One person next to our cabin seems to bring more food up than he takes down. However, that has not bothered us. We are having a delightful trip and have met some very nice people. It is now Church time. Will finish this after church. They seem to be slow in starting church so shall finish this letter. They church in the ladies' lounge room each Sunday. I am writing this letter in that room. I have brought us calm to Sunday as each day in a boat is about the same. Well, we had a Lutheran minister from some church in the U.S. He preached a good sermon. Well, I have written about enough for one letter. Not to have written anything at all. You must remember me having been on the water at least part of every day since July 8th. Hope all of you are well as usual.

With love, Ernest & Clare

The copy of this letter in Mac's archives in Phoenix is clipped to another letter, which appears to have been sent in the same envelope:

Tuesday. We will arrive at Plymouth sometime tomorrow night and leave boat early Thursday A.M., which suits us fine as we wanted to go to London in the daytime. There will be a boat train there waiting. There are a great many interesting people on board this ship, as every other ship. It is nice to meet them and get their ideas about things. We are going to bring birthday presents back with us. This is wishing you a happy birthday for the present.[2]

Mac's papers also confirm how much this trip influenced his worldview:

> A boat trip was very educational in those days, because one met people from other countries, and in visiting with them, I learned a great deal. Someone on the ship told us where we could get a room to stay in London and other places for a reasonable amount of money. We met some people from South America. They rather resented our referring to ourselves as "Americans," as though we were the only Americans. I visited sufficient old churches and cathedrals on the trip to last me the rest of my life, if merely visiting them would help my religion.

The SS *George Washington* was used by Woodrow Wilson a decade earlier to attend the Versailles Peace Conference. While there is no documentation about the ship's origin and history in Mac's archives or his books, it is likely Mac was familiar with the vessel. His voracious interest in history and his service in World War I strongly suggests he knew the connection between their trip on the *George Washington* and President Wilson's earlier trip. It was built as an ocean liner in 1908 in Bremen, Germany, and was named after George Washington, the first president of the United States. The ship was later known as USS *George Washington* (ID-3018) and the USAT *George Washington* in service of the United States Navy and United States Army, respectively, during World War I. In the interwar period, she reverted to her original name of SS *George Washington*.

When the SS *George Washington* was launched in 1908, she was the largest German-built steamship and the third-largest ship in the world. Her designers emphasized comfort over speed. Although Mac and Clare did not sail first class, they surely visited with "upper class passengers," and enjoyed how sumptuously appointed she was. The ship carried 2,900 passengers on her maiden voyage in January 1909 to New York. In June 1911, the *George Washington* was the largest ship to participate in the Coronation Fleet Review by the United Kingdom's newly crowned king, George V.

All ocean liners took a similar track from New York to England in the 1920s. The same route they took in 1912. The *George Washington*'s log confirms an eerie coincidence. On April 14, 1912, she passed a particularly large iceberg south of the Grand Banks of Newfoundland and radioed a warning to all ships in the area, including the White Star Line ocean liner, the *Titanic*. Mac's letters do not mention this connection, but Mac no doubt knew where the *Titanic* sank. Likely, he and others on the ship talked about the *Titanic* as they sailed the same track across the Atlantic.

At the outbreak of World War I, the SS *George Washington* was interned by the then-neutral United States, until the country entered the conflict in April 1917. It was used as a troop transport by the U.S. Navy. Commissioned as USS *George Washington* (ID-3018), she sailed with her first load of American troops to Europe in December 1917. But for Mac's near-death experience 1918, Mac might well have been assigned to the USS *George Washington* as he commenced his naval enlistment.

Once docked in Plymouth, Mac and Clare visited London, and the Celtic capitals of Belfast, Dublin, and Edinburgh, where Mac stocked up on "McFarland Clan ties." From England, they traveled first to Germany, then to Belgium, and finally to Paris. They enjoyed their first plane ride, a short flight between Brussels and Rheims.

Mac had booked a French ship from Paris to New York, but for some reason, the ship did not depart. He rebooked on the SS *Leviathan*. But it was oversold, so they did not have a cabin together on the return trip to New York. But, Mac said, "it was a first class ship and we thought it was beautiful." After almost eight weeks in Europe, they were ready to go home. The SS *Leviathan* was another German-designed ocean liner, which regularly crossed the North Atlantic from 1914 to 1934. She was one of three sister ships built for Germany's Hamburg America Line for their transatlantic passenger service. And, like several other German ships, she sailed for less than a year before her early career was halted by the start of World War I. In 1917, she was seized by the U.S. government and renamed the SS *Leviathan*. She would become known by this name for the majority of her seafaring years, both as a troopship during World War I and later as the flagship of the United States Lines. Mac described her as "overcrowded with 2,600 passengers and 1,000 crew. They assigned us to separate group rooms, where we all suffered sea sickness."

Mac wryly said, "I did not miss a meal and returned all of them." While sailing the Pacific on the first leg of the trip, Mac and Clare were spared seasickness on the abnormally calm waters. But on the last leg, Mac's letters focused on the fact that the "Atlantic is rougher than the Pacific."

This trip changed Mac's view of the world. It did little for Clare, who spent much of the trip in their cabin. Mac rigorously sought out the company of fellow travelers, particularly foreigners, rubbing shoulders with them. He plied them for information on their governments, societies, law, farms, business, taxes, and profits and how they were faring the world depression. He mentally filed away reams of disparate information on European social, political, and economic practices, theories, and problems. At home, Mac had always been a people person. Accordingly, his interaction with European cultures quickly became what he called a "constructive passion." This trip established many of his lifelong travel patterns.

But still, the deaths of their children must have been on their minds every day. Even with his daily mingling with other passengers from many countries, Mac closely watched after Clare. He said in a letter to home, "Clare has stood the trip pretty well although she has gotten pretty tired at times. I think as a whole, it has been good for her. I believe it has helped get her mind off things."

Mac's biographer wrote, "While the voyage may have alleviated Clare's mental depression, it is debatable whether it had such a salubrious effect on her physical well-being. Mac's letters are filled with detail on the hardships of packing, unpacking, and making travel deadlines via boat, train, plane, car, subway and cab, particularly in the big cities."[3]

There is nothing in the McMillan biography, Mac's autobiography, or in the Arizona State Archives about the couple having more children or even discussing the topic. Nor is there mention of the talks Mac and Clare must have had about losing their children. Nonetheless, knowing the kind of people they were, it is fair to assume they talked about more children.

Docking in New York in September 1929 marked the final leg of their ten-week trip to Europe. They could not have anticipated the stock market crash just a month later in New York. As was to become his custom, Mac bought a new automobile direct off the factory line to save the substantial shipping fees back to Arizona.[4] He and Clare drove back across the continent "soaking in the atmosphere of the eastern United States." Neither had seen that part of America before. They arrived in Florence a week later, as Mac put it, "a weary but satisfied couple."

From October 1929 to December 1930, little is known how Mac and Clare rebuilt their family life, other than that they were again engaged in much of what was happening in Florence that year. Then, just as winter was settling in on the Gila River Valley, the utterly unthinkable struck again. Their third child, Juliet, was stillborn on December 5, 1930. Clare died eight days later. There was no birth certificate for Juliet. Clare's death certificate unceremoniously lists her cause of death as "pneumonia—contributory advanced pregnancy."

Everyone in Florence was deeply impacted by the McFarland family tragedy. Clare's services at the Presbyterian church was the largest affair in the history of Florence. There was no official obituary filed, but the newspaper article filed the day after she died read:

> [S]he has lived in our midst, keenly interested in church and community work, an inspiration to all with whom she came in contact. Few people are as attuned to the beautiful as Clare McFarland was. Whether a daughter, sister, wife, or mother she was unfailingly sweet, gentle and loving. So modest was she that only to her closest friends did she reveal the quality of the charm, and the depth of her culture. Only in the best of the arts, in her surroundings did she choose, and from others she attracted only the good qualities, either ignoring or covering up gross. She has lived this life before us and we are all better that she has lived.

Clare and Juliet were laid to rest flanking the graves from the previous year of William Ernest and Jean Clare. The cemetery contrasted bleakness and beauty. Mac's religious beliefs and decorum were nearly shattered by the enormity and the utter suddenness of the tragedies. Neither he nor his closest friends and family could believe Mac had lost his wife and all three children in less than twenty-two months. There were undoubtedly many times when nothing made sense to him. The public record is largely silent about how Mac dealt with tragedy. In retrospect, it may be that no one in Arizona except his mother could have made the connection to Mac's own near-death experience in 1918 and the deaths of his wife and three children just twelve years later.

A few months after the burial ceremonies, a townsman found him hopelessly inebriated, and despondent beneath the bridge crossing the Gila River, watching the high winter waters pass as he perhaps contemplated suicide.[5]

Because the written history of Mac's loss is so sparse, his family tragedy can only be imagined by his grandchildren, the prodigy of his second, life-saving marriage. However, his later writings and his Oklahoma family's long experience with the inevitability of death do, at least inferentially, suggest how he reacted and what coping mechanisms he chose. Mac alternated between desperately trying to avoid the pain he felt and the feeling of helplessness when confronted with such bewildering tragedy in a twenty-two-month span.

His comprehensive studies in history, political science, and moral philosophy likely made him acutely aware of the high maternal and infant mortality rates in America in the 1930s. Puerperal fever and antisepsis were the most common causes of maternal mortality in the United States before 1935. The Florence hospital record is silent about Clare McFarland, other than the general reference to "pneumonia complicated by advanced pregnancy." Fever accounted for almost 40 percent of infant and maternal death in both rural and urban areas in America at the time.

Mac knew all too well the risks rural families faced with childbirth. Other Florence men had lost children, wives, and mothers. From counseling some of them as clients in probate cases and through his work at the First Presbyterian Church, Mac knew that death was an event every family faced. But facing four deaths in such a short time was dramatically different. No other young father and husband could possibly relate to Mac's experience. No one knew that Mac himself had faced death from influenza and pneumonia a decade years earlier. No one could have guessed he'd given up on Oklahoma in favor of Arizona largely because of his near-death in middle America.

No other town in Arizona bore witness to such a twenty-two-month tragedy by any of their hardworking families. The tragedy affected everyone, but it could have consumed him. However, with Florence's help, his grief was relatively short lived. The business, legal, farming, and church people in Florence rescued Mac. He hung on, just as he had done for more than a year in the hospital in Great Lakes, Illinois, when his own life hung in the balance. That singular experience in a U.S. Navy hospital likely came back not to haunt him, but to *guide* him.

A homily is often told in situations like the one Mac faced. It could be a rural myth, but it shows up often enough to suggest it was spread from one church to another across the western states. It's about a bird on a branch. After a long flight through a great storm, the bird landed on a stout branch in a large oak tree. Like all tree branches, it offered the bird a fine view below as well as safety from dangerous animals. But the storm wasn't over, and the branch began to bend and creak. The bird thought it might break, but he knew the storm would eventually blow itself out. He just stuck to the branch, keeping his beak into the wind. Like all smart birds, this one knew that even without the branch, he could still fly. He could remain safe through the power of his own two wings. And he knew there were other branches in other trees.

Given what is known now about Mac, that might have been what Mac thought once he fought his way through the grief of losing nearly everything that was important to him as the decade of the thirties came to Florence, Arizona. He was just thirty-five years old.

Mac took everything in life head-on, with the possible exception of Clare's death. In his autobiography, he almost casually mentioned her death, as though it were an afterthought. Almost fifty years had passed between Clare's death and Mac's writing of his autobiography. Even so, fifty years was not enough for Mac to open that first great tragedy of his life. He barely touched his own death in 1919 and only referenced Clare's death as a parenthetical reference in a paragraph about their cruise from New York to Europe.

"While we were in Germany, we visited a couple we had met on the boat. They had decided to stay in Germany to take care of their parents. It was a close acquaintance, and when Clare passed away later, they wrote me a letter of sympathy and enclosed a dollar bill. They said, 'this is our last American dollar. Buy some flowers for her grave.'"

One thing Mac didn't lose was his faith in the law, his allegiance to the court, and his clients. He and Tommy Fulbright ramped up their law practice. Just four months later, Mac became embroiled in the Winnie Ruth Judd case. That bizarre court battle would narrow his view of the kind of law he wanted to practice, just as the European trip had broadened his view of world culture.[6]

11

Mac and Henry Fountain Ashurst in the 1930s

Mac was forty-one when he visited Hoover Dam in the late fall of 1935; Henry Fountain Ashurst was sixty-one. Mac had been a county judge for one year, and Ashurst had been a United States senator for twenty-one years. Mac was starting to think about Ashurst's job.

The year 1935 was a metaphor for Mac and what he would soon become. The Hoover Dam was the biggest dam anyone had ever seen in Arizona. Named after President Herbert Hoover, whom Franklin Delano Roosevelt had defeated in 1932, the dam was huge, and it was also a huge defeat. Mac's sense of the scale of the dam was not recorded, but by 1935, Roosevelt and Mac were both on the way to even bigger things. There was nothing bigger than Hoover Dam. A nationally prominent newspaper reporter recorded the basic logistics and metrics. It was so grand, he wrote, that the notion was akin to "thumbing your nose at Mother Nature."[1]

Just a few years earlier, the site of the dam was a river that roared and hissed at the bottom of a deep notch cut between ugly, tumbling, black hills. Bereft of vegetation and benighted by sharp-edged volcanic ash, it was sited in a canyon which produced 120-degree days in summer and blistering cold come wintertime. But in 1935, it boasted the world's biggest dam—six hundred feet through at the base, towering almost two-thirds as high as the

Empire State Building. The engineers of the dam knew then that it would take ten years to fill the lake behind it—one that would be 8 miles wide, 115 miles long, and deep enough to cover all of Arizona with a foot of clear Rocky Mountain water.

It was by far the largest piece of masonry ever attempted, weighing six million tons. It had many purposes: flood control, irrigation, silt control, water supply, and electricity. It would beget aqueducts, bridges, roads, and carry one billion dollars of water per day to Los Angeles and Arizona though low deserts and high mountains. The primary aqueduct would cost sixty million dollars *more* than the dam itself. Behind only the Panama Canal, it was the world's greatest engineering feat. And because it would change Arizona forever, it would fuel Mac's drive from an obscure, small-county Arizona judgeship to the pinnacle of power in the United States Senate in less time than it took to build the dam. Arizona, unlike other parts of the country, had a greater need for water than it had for politics. But water politics would come to play a central role in Mac's rise to national prominence.

In 1935, many people all over America were disheartened because, after three years of the New Deal, utopia was not at hand. This mood made people more susceptible to political demagogues and prophets then they had been in earlier hopeless days of the Great Depression. H. G. Wells said, "the New Deal has not gone far enough fast enough."

But for Henry F. Ashurst, the year had gone very well. By 1935, he'd been Arizona's senior member of the U.S. Senate for more than two decades, having been elected in 1912 by the Arizona legislature as one of the first two senators from Arizona. It was not much of a surprise, since Ashurst, as Arizona's youngest legislative speaker, presided over Arizona's first constitutional convention. In 1916, he was elected by popular vote and again in 1922, 1928, and 1934. In hindsight, it's fair to say that Ashurst never saw Mac coming. Ashurst had easily won the general election in 1934. Just six years later, Mac beat him easily in the 1940 Democratic primary. Ashurst, an eloquent speaker, is famous for how he reflected on the experience of his only political defeat:

> The first half-hour, you imagine that the earth has slipped from beneath your feet and that the stars above your head have paled and faded, and in your heart you wonder how the Senate will do without you, and how the country will get

along without you. But, within another hour, there comes a peace and joy to be envied by the world's greatest philosopher."[2]

Just two years before, shortly after Roosevelt's win over Hoover, middle America faced the great black blizzard of November 11, 1933. It darkened the sky from Chicago to Albany and was prelude to the disaster that became the Great Depression. During 1934 and 1935, many thousands of square miles were laid to waste. The people in the Midwest were set adrift upon desperate migrations across the Great Plains. Many blamed the migrations on the combination of light rainfall, high sun, huge winds, and overgrazed grasslands. Cattle drives from ranches to slaughter houses made it all worse. For decades, homesteaders had been trying to wring a living from semiarid soil. They did it with wheat as tractors for large-scale farming became available. The Great Plains turned to sod as the covering that protected the land was plowed on a grand scale. Midwesterners fled west from what some called the new Sahara. Between 1933 and 1935, Californians and Arizonans watched as the remarkable influx of families in old trucks and even older jalopies rumbled along Highway 66 from east to west, all in need of jobs and water.

Despite all of America's vast resources, the land in the 1930s was in critical condition. On Armistice Day in 1933, the Great Plains were swept from Texas to Canada with a wall of dirt no one's eyes could penetrate. "When the wind died and people could see again, there were no fields, only sand drifting into mounds and eddies. In thousands of farmyards, fences, machinery, and trees were gone, buried and the roofs of sheds stuck out through drifts deeper than a man is tall."[3]

In the American Midwest, which had always been a land of promise, agriculture had long been partly industrialized. Huge farms were in control of absentee owners—banks or corporations—and were accustomed to depending upon the labor of migratory "fruit tramps," who had formerly been mostly Mexicans, Japanese, and other foreign migrants, but were becoming increasingly American. Wave after wave of migrants headed west, to Arizona and California; the labor force became glutted, earnings were low, and jobs became so scarce that groups of poverty-stricken families would be found squatting in makeshift "Hoovervilles."[4]

Between Mac's ascension to the bench in Pinal County in 1934 and the Hoover Dam's dedication in 1935, Americans and Arizonans started to feel like the Depression was behind them—not far behind, but at least no longer looming with black clouds and blacker moods. The following year, 1936, passed without as much economic dread. Roosevelt's budget message in January 1937 spoke to a continuing recovery and the safety that American business promised. Relief rolls were cut, and many public works projects were reduced. But money men in dapper suits would soon frown. The economy took a nosedive in the fall. By March 1938, AT&T, which had been selling for $170 per share, was down sixty bucks per share. The national recovery was in peril. Investors slowed down, government spending lagged, the treasury secretary persuaded the president to balance the budget. Business leaders cut production. Two million men were let go in a few months from jobs they believed were secure. A new disaster welled up: recession. No more speculative boom in stocks or real estate, no tightness in credit, no expansion of capacity to make capital goods.

Mac was both a farmer and a county judge in the midthirties. As the recession deepened in 1938, angry national voices from big business and conservative politicians blamed it on Democrats; this was a "Roosevelt Depression." The president quit trying to balance the budget and plowed ahead with heaving government spending. In April 1938, he asked Congress to appropriate three billion dollars for relief, public works, housing, flood control, and other recovery efforts. Senator Ashurst voted for all of them. Business, by the spring of 1938, showed signs of recovery. In late June, the stock market showed new life.

The Politics of the Late 1930s

It is the case today that the United States is the unquestioned world leader. Foreign policy is important.[5] But in the 1930s, particularly the late 1930s, foreign policy was subordinate, especially in the Roosevelt administration. "No risk, no commitments," was the White House's motto.[6] That would all change on December 7, 1941. However, before the 1940 election season opened, America could fairly be called ambivalent, with a pronounced drift toward isolationism. There were neutrality debates, pacifist sentiment, and a doubtful public. In 1937, most college students supported no U.S. role in what many knew was a coming war in Europe. Nineteen out of twenty people in a 1937 poll answered "no" to the question of whether they thought the U.S. should enter another war. To make the politics worse, or better depending on whether you were a Republican or a Democrat, there was a definite distaste for military spending. *Fortune* magazine reported that America had "165,000 soldiers, 67 generals, enough rifles for one regiment, and a handful of effective tanks."[7] To add salt to the military wound, the army's plan (as set by Congress) for new equipment in the coming year was limited to purchasing 1,870 new rifles. Some who were to run for national office in 1940, including Mac, might have thought the American people were the prize idiots of all time. But hindsight was even more lacking than foresight. In the late 1930s, America wanted to evade responsibility beyond its borders. That's understandable, because in the early 1930s it experienced the Great Depression and as the late 1930s, it faced the Great Recession. It's understandable because, of all the great nations, America had the most naïve view of the role of force in international affairs. In World War I, the war Mac missed because he nearly died in a naval hospital in Illinois, 8,000,000 soldiers and an estimated 12,000,000 civilians died. Germany suffered 1,700,000 killed and more than 4,000,000 wounded. France experienced 1,000,000 deaths and more than 4,200,000 wounded. And while the war was difficult for the United States, the country only lost 50,000 men. America had risen to greatness, essentially, without engaging in Europe's large-scale war. The power politics in Europe played little role in American success.

Dexter Perkins said it best:

> Without experience in the politics of Europe, Americans viewed the competitions of Europe as a sinister game which they neither desired nor felt compelled to play . . . it had seen, just as President Roosevelt entered office, the nations of the Old World repudiate their indebtedness to the United States . . . [and] it was easy to believe, as President Hoover had, that America would have emerged much sooner from the Depression if it had not been for the European economic crisis of 1931 and if the wrangling nations of the Old World had not deepened their own economic difficulties by political rivalries, if they had not

intensified their own misery by folly and the game of power. There is something unique about the political and economic order of the United States—only contamination could come from closer association with the wicked world outside American borders.[8]

12

Mac and the Winnie Ruth Judd Case, 1933

Mac likely thought he'd never see another sanity trial once the Eva Dugan trial ended in her execution on February 21, 1930. But three years later, he took on another sanity trial. It involved another woman convicted of murder; she was awaiting execution in the Arizona State Penitentiary across the road from his office in Florence, Arizona. But this time, he was on the other side of the courtroom. He'd successfully argued to send Eva Dugan to the gallows. Now his job was to craft an argument that would keep Winnie Ruth Judd out of the gas chamber.

At the time, Arizona's death penalty history was marked by inconsistency. The Arizona State Penitentiary was built in Florence in 1910. By law, all executions had to be carried out there. Jose Lopez was the first prisoner executed there on January 5, 1910. He was followed by eight other men. But in 1916, an initiative measure went into legal effect eliminating the death penalty for first-degree murder convictions. Two years later, on December 5, 1918, the death penalty was restored. That led to nineteen executions over the next twelve years, including the debacle of Eva Dugan's beheading. Eventually, the law was changed, and two brothers, Manuel and Fred Hernandez, were executed by lethal gas on July 6, 1934.

Winne Ruth Judd's sanity hearing came before the Pinal County Superior Court in that four-year gap between Eva Dugan's hanging and the Hernandez brothers' gassing. But at the time of her hearing, Arizona was still executing by hanging.[1]

Today, the most knowledgeable person in Arizona on Winnie Ruth Judd is author and investigative reporter Jana Bommersbach. Her book *The Trunk Murderess: Winnie Ruth Judd* is the definitive authority on the case. She lays out what she and many others believe really happened. "Winnie Ruth Judd became a household name across America as Arizona made her pay with one of the longest sentences this country has ever seen: thirty-eight years, eleven months, and twenty-two days. The press labeled her 'The Trunk Murderess and the Tiger Woman.' She was convicted and sentenced to hang, and then declared insane, and saved from the gallows by only seventy-two hours." This was thanks to Mac and Tommy.

Ruth Judd was born in 1905 in Indiana. Seventeen years later, she married a man more than twenty years her senior and moved to Mexico with him. William C. Judd, a physician, was reportedly a morphine addict because of injuries he suffered in World War I. They moved back to Phoenix, but by 1930, they were separated. While working as a governess for a wealthy Phoenix family, she fell in love with a married man named Jack Halloran. The press dubbed Halloran a playboy and philanderer. Ruth worked at the Grunow Medical Clinic, where she met Agnes LeRoi, an X-ray technician. Agnes had another friend, Hedvig Samuelson. Ruth lived with Agnes and Hedvig for a few months but moved out when problems broke out among them. She often visited with them after moving to her own apartment.

The Phoenix police believed that Ruth murdered Agnes and Hedvig after a fight broke out over Halloran's affections during the night of October 16, 1931. The police reported that Ruth used a .25-caliber handgun to kill her two friends. Then, she and an accomplice dismembered Hedvig's body and put the head, torso, and lower legs into a black steamer trunk. They also stuck Agnes's body in that trunk. Hedvig's upper legs went into a beige trunk, and other unnamed body parts were stuffed into a hatbox.

On October 18, Ruth arrived at the Union Station in Los Angeles with her two trunks, the hatbox, and several valises. A baggage man noticed what he thought was blood dripping from one trunk. He asked her to open it, but

> **WANTED**
> For Double Murder
> Murdered and mutilated two young women at Phoenix Ariz. Oct. 16, 1931
> WINNIE RUTH JUDD —
> Mrs. Judd will no doubt represent herself to e a professional nurse —— She has a very leasing personality, rather slender build, lim legs and thick hair —
>
> Age 25 — Height 5ft 7 inches — Weight 125 — -yes Blue grey and large — Hair Light brown —
>
> Arrest and notify Geo. O. Brisboise Chief of Police

Wanted Poster for Winnie Ruth Judd, ca. 1931.

she said she did not have a key. Then she and her brother, Burton McKinnell, who lived in Los Angeles, left in his car. The railroad officials called the police, who traced the car from its license plate. The black trunk revealed Hedvig Samuelson's body, neatly cut into three pieces to make it easier to pack. The beige trunk revealed someone's upper legs. The hatbox held a kit of surgeon's tools, a scalpel, and a .25-caliber automatic pistol. Judd's purse, which she left on the luggage cart, revealed one lead bullet and two empty shells. The next day, the police found Ruth, arrested her, and held her for Phoenix officers to come get her.

When the Phoenix police went to the bungalow, they allowed neighbors and reporters to enter, destroying crime scene evidence. The next day, the bungalow owner placed an ad in the *Phoenix Evening Gazette* offering ten-cent tours per person. Before Judd was returned to Phoenix, hundreds of curiosity seekers visited the scene. The police theory was that both women were shot while asleep in their beds, but the mattresses were missing when the police got there. One was eventually found, miles away, but without bloodstains. The other was never found.

The prosecutors charged Judd only with one of the two murders, saving the second case for a trial if the first one proved unsuccessful. Judge Howard C. Speakerman presided over the case. Judd's legal team, paid for by William Randolph Hearst, argued two theories, self-defense and insanity. Judge Speakerman told the jury the law on insanity was a "right and wrong" rule, rather than the "irresistible impulse" rule used in other states. Arizona law, he instructed the jury, presumes that every person charged with a crime is sane and was sane at the time of the crime. The only way to avoid that presumption is for the defense to prove the defendant was unable to perceive and know the criminal act was wrong. He also instructed the jury that if they believed the defendant was sane, the law implies deliberation and premeditation from the circumstances of the killing. As long as the defendant knew the nature and quality of her act, and that it was wrong, she is subject to punishment for the act.

At trial, the prosecutors proved the .25-caliber automatic owned by Judd had fired the empty shells found in her purse. That gun was also matched to one of the bullets found in Agnes LeRoi's body. They also offered a document referred to during the trial as the "drain letter." It had been recovered in the Broadway department store in Los Angeles from the ladies' restroom, just after Judd had apparently used it. The letter was addressed to Ruth's husband and recited episodes from her muddled life and her account of what led up to killing the two victims. It also contained what the Arizona Supreme Court dubbed "a graphic, if somewhat incoherent description of what happened at the time of the killing." Judd did not testify in her own defense. The only evidence offered by her lawyers related to her insanity defense.

She had arrived in Los Angeles with a gunshot wound to her hand. Some evidence established indicated that the wound came as she struggled with Miss Samuelson. Other witnesses said they saw Judd with her hand bandaged before the night of the killings. While the trial was hard fought, the circus atmosphere in which it was tried and the salacious nature of the evidence likely contributed to the guilty verdict and her death penalty.

The murder trial brimmed over with what Jana Bommersbach called "social taboos—a totally unacceptable love affair, the threat of deadly and incurable syphilis, snide rumors of lesbianism, outright declarations that these were 'party girls,'—the nice term used in the thirties for prostitutes. Add that," Bommersbach reported, "to the widespread allegations that one of Phoenix's most prominent businessmen was knee-deep in the crime—allegations widely reported in out-of-state newspapers, but excused and dismissed by the press at home. Then, mix in the mysterious shadow of

William Randolph Hearst, the most powerful newspaper publisher for the day, and the intervention of First Lady Eleanor Roosevelt. The case was not just another murder mystery. It was a slice of Arizona and America at a most vulnerable moment: exactly two years after the stock market crash that ushered in the Great Depression, twelve years into the disastrous ban on 'spirits' knows as Prohibition, and a time when media excess would be forever defined and remain a constant embarrassment for every journalist who came after."

Two primary issues were raised on appeal to the Arizona Supreme Court: whether a letter from Judd describing her view of the killings should have been admitted and whether the instruction on sanity was proper. Collateral issues regarding a juror's answers to a lawyer's questions during the voir dire portion of the trial and whether evidence about the other woman's murder should have been admitted by the trial judge were not persuasive. The ten-page opinion affirming the lower court's verdict and death sentence was unanimous. Justices Ross and Lockwood concurred with Judge Joseph S. Jencks, who wrote the opinion.

Mac was not involved in either the first trial or the appeal. His sole role was as her defense lawyer in her 1933 sanity hearing. Mac recalled that role well in his autobiography: "I spoke of having the unpleasant job of defending Eva Dugan's sanity while I was county attorney. I had another case I did not enjoy. Tom Fulbright and I handled the sanity case of Winnie Ruth Judd after her murder conviction was upheld by the Supreme Court. The warden had certified that in his opinion she was insane." Warden A. G. Walker was not alone in that opinion.

On April 12, 1933, W. C. Thurman, known as Bill to his friends, filed a formal petition in the Pinal County Superior Court under section 5122 of the Arizona Revised Code (1928) seeking a "sanity hearing."[2] The law required a trial by jury to determine whether the prisoner was sane or insane. It was Thurman's job to prosecute the case for sanity and Mac's job to defend on the basis of insanity. The petition stated the obvious—the prisoner had been convicted by a Maricopa county jury of murder and sentenced to death—her final date for execution was set by the Arizona Supreme Court for April 21, 1933. The sentence was to be carried out by hanging. The larger context was left unsaid in the petition—did the State of Arizona really want to hang another woman after the beheading of Eva Dugan just three years earlier? And who might answer that question better than Mac? He had been the prosecutor back then and won the sanity case against Dugan—and now he was the defense lawyer trying to establish Winnie Ruth Judd's insanity so they could avoid hanging her. Could anyone afford another beheading? No little irony there, especially for such a small county as Pinal.

The petition clarified why they needed another sanity hearing. The warden himself swore out an affidavit on Judd's behalf. Warden Walker's affidavit read, "there is good reason to believe Winnie Ruth Judd has become insane, that your affiant bases his information upon the opinion of different physicians, and from his own observations, and the observations of others as communicated to him."

Judge E. L. Green received the county attorney's petition on April 12, 1933, just nine days before the scheduled execution date. He knew all too well what everyone in Florence was worried about—another woman strapped to a hanging board—another possible beheading. But Judge Green's succinct order ignored that sense of foreboding while recognizing that time was of the essence. "It appearing from said petition that there are sufficient grounds upon which to cause an inquiry into the sanity of the said Winnie Ruth Judd, it is ORDERED that the sanity of Winnie Ruth Judd be inquired into, and that a jury be forthwith summoned and impaneled on the 14th day of April, 1933." The lawyers, witnesses, doctors, and prison guards had two days to prepare and resolve a prisoner's sanity just seven days before her death warrant would put her back the same platform, tied to the same hanging board, and facing a much larger crowd, each fearing another execution malfunction.

Fourteen witnesses were subpoenaed, including five doctors and two members of Judd's family. At that time, Arizona law put the burden of proving insanity on the prisoner. As Judd's lawyer, Mac had to overcome the legal presumption that every person is presumed to be sane. That meant he had to meet a specific statutory test. He had to prove Winnie Ruth Judd became insane *after* her delivery from the trial court to the state prison. It was a unique time period because the jury had rejected her insanity defense in 1931. That rejection had been affirmed by the Arizona Supreme Court.

But Mac was a true insider. He had successfully prosecuted Eva Dugan's sanity hearing and had the written jury instructions in his file from that case. He knew Judge Green would give the same exact set of instructions to the Judd jury. Those instructions laid out a clear path for him if he was to establish Judd's present insanity. He reread the set of instructions used three years earlier in Dugan.

> Gentlemen of the jury, the question which you must decide in this case is whether Eva Dugan, since her delivery to the Superintendent of the Arizona State Prison to await execution under sentence of the death penalty has become insane. You are instructed, gentlemen of the jury, that every person is presumed to be sane until the contrary is proven. You are therefore instructed that in the case, the burden is upon Eva Dugan to prove by a preponderance of the evidence that she has become insane since her delivery and is at the present time insane within the definition which I will now read to you. Has Eva Dugan sufficient intelligence to understand the proceedings against her, what she was tried for, the purpose of her punishment, the impending fate which awaits her; and a sufficient understanding to know any fact which might exist which would make her punishment unjust or unlawful, and sufficient intelligence to convey such information to her attorneys in court.

All Mac had to do was prove Judd's insanity in the same way he had proved Dugan sane. In his autobiography, Mac described the odd circumstances that brought him and Tommy into the case:

> The case had been hard fought from the beginning. We took it solely because her father—a retired minister, stooped over with years, whose hair had turned white partly because of concern over his daughter—came to us and said he was proud we were going to handle her case, even though he didn't have any money to pay us. Someone had told him I had agreed to take the case. This was misinformation, however. The other lawyers had only told him they would ask us. We didn't the heart to turn him down.[3]

In 1933, Mac did something in the Judd case no lawyer could get away with today. As he put it in his autobiography,

I told him [Judd's father] I would enter the case on one condition—that I would not talk with Ruth Judd before, or during the trial. I did not want to put myself in the position of trying to determine her sanity for myself. I wanted to try the case on evidence presented rather than from a personal interview. I considered it my duty to do so. It was hard-fought, but the jury returned the verdict in our favor. I remember some of my speech to the jury. It was just after Easter Sunday, and I told the jury that we had just passed through the Easter season, and reminded them that the thief had asked forgiveness of Christ, while they were on the cross. I said that that was what we were asking for Ruth Judd. If she was to be executed, it would be at a time when she was sane and able to ask for forgiveness. A reporter from the *Los Angeles Times* told me my speech to the jury won the case.[4]

Today, a lawyer defending a client but refusing to talk to her before or during trial would be subjected to serious rebuke by the bar association. But Mac's position was likely not known to the bar nor was the act questioned by the judge.

After the verdict the next day, I decided to go to see Ruth. She was all dressed up and told me what a wonderful speech I had made. I said to her, "How do you know, you're crazy." She laughed at that, but in my conversation with her regarding the night of the "trunk murders," I questioned her about one of the people who was at the party that night. Her answers were such that I was convinced she really did have a streak of insanity. Also, some of the evidence presented was that she would tell people about having a wonderful family and about her children. Of course I had no way of knowing then whether she made the statements, but it was our duty to present the evidence. After the verdict was rendered, one of the businessman in Florence told he had gone to the Grunow Clinic in Phoenix, where she was the receptionist. He said that she told him she had a wonderful family, and all about her four children. She, of course, never had any children. Her husband, Dr. Judd had had an abortion performed on her in Mexico City. While she was at the Arizona State Hospital, she showed a deep affection for children in her work assisting in their care. Incidentally, Winnie Ruth, who had a record of escaping from the state mental hospital almost at will, wrote me a 37-page letter when I was elected

Governor in which she stated she would never give me any trouble. I never answered the letter, but she kept her word. She did not try to escape while I was governor. The contents of that letter further convinced me she had what we call a "streak of insanity."[5]

On April 22, 1933, Judge Green signed a formal judgment, finding as a matter of fact and law that Judd was insane and ordering that "she be forthwith delivered to the superintendent of the Arizona State Hospital for the Insane at Phoenix, Arizona, and kept there in safe confinement until her reason is restored."

Little was heard from or about Judd for twenty years. On March 14, 1953, Judd's guardian, Elizabeth Harvey, petitioned the Pinal County Superior Court to reexamine Judd's mental status asserting "she should no longer be held and detained at the hospital because she is not insane." Harvey asked for a hearing on the matter. In one of those "only in Arizona moments," Pinal County Attorney T. J. Mahoney opposed the petition "for the reasons and on the grounds that the petition does not state a cause of action." Mr. Mahoney's motion was heard and granted by Judge Porter Murray on March 27, 1953. While the record is still under seal in the probate division of the Pinal County Superior Court, it is fair to assume that the state prison did not want Judd back. The state hospital did not want to give her up. Only Judd's appointed guardian wanted a hearing. Had Harvey's case succeeded, Judd could not have stayed in the state hospital, but her conviction for murder would still be in effect. It's fair to assume that Judd would be better off sane in the insane asylum than she would have been sane in prison.

Winnie Ruth Judd's story did not end with the failed 1953 petition to have her declared sane. She escaped from the state hospital six times. On her sixth escape, which lasted for six and a half years, she lived in the San Francisco area under the name of Marian Lane. She was taken back to the state hospital in 1968. Three years later, after much legal wrangling by her new Arizona lawyer, Larry Debus, she was released on parole on December 22, 1971. In 1983, Arizona discharged her. She died in 1998 at age ninety-three.

Because of the Dugan debacle and his own family tragedies, Mac took solace at having helped to save Winnie Ruth Judd's life. He later said he firmly believed she was mentally ill after having finally meeting her and talking to her.[6]

Today the law is clear. The Eighth Amendment prohibits the execution of insane prisoners. Prisoners sentenced to death have a constitutional right not to be executed if they are insane at the time of execution. The recognition of the constitutional rights of insane prisoners is significant because it requires full due process standards for determining sanity and for dealing with allegations of insanity. The old "sanity" hearings in Arizona might not have afforded prisoners full due process. Arguably, that reality is proved by contrasting the way Eva Dugan was executed and Winnie Ruth Judd was not. Both were afforded due process, thanks to Mac.

13

Mac Runs for Pinal County Judge Twice, 1930 and 1934

Mac explained his first run for Pinal County Superior Court in practical terms. He had just finished the Eva Dugan sanity trial, and felt bad about the experience. "I became tired of pushing people into the penitentiary." So he ran for election to the Pinal County Superior Court judgeship in the upcoming 1930 elections and lost by a mere 106 votes. The incumbent judge, E. L. Greene, got 1,464 votes, while Mac received 1,358.[1] Everyone thought Judge Greene did a good job. So did Mac. But he bided his time, practicing law with Tommy Fulbright and trying every day to live life without Clare and the children.

In 1934, he ran against E. L. Greene once again. This time, the Florence newspaper did not endorse either candidate, saying, "Both men are good capable men worthy of your support." Mac emphasized his fourteen-year county residency, courtroom experience, and education at Stanford Law School. This time, he won in a lopsided vote of 2,543 to 1,542. His four years of private practice in Florence from 1930 to 1934 earned him a 1,001-vote win. That same year, Senator Henry Ashurst was reelected to the U.S. Senate, and B. B. Mour took over the governor's office, bringing Governor Hunt's fifty-five-year career in Arizona politics to an end.

Mac reminisced about this race in his 1979 autobiography:

> In 1934, I was confronted with the question of whether I would again make the race for Superior Court Judge. In four years during the depression, I had built a good law practice, and had acquired property which gave me the funds for successful farming in later years. However, I was "goaded" by my desire to become Judge of the Superior Court, and particularly, since I had lost to become judge by only eighty votes. So I made the race in 1934, was nominated in the primary and ran in the general election without opposition . . . I was always glad that I had made the race. I don't believe there is any position in life that gave me more pleasure than walking out to the bench for the first time in January 1935. I felt I had made a step up in my profession.

The year 1934 was definitely one for Democrats in Arizona as well as the rest of the country. Roosevelt's New Deal campaign had impressed voters nationwide. Arizona was essentially a one-party state. The Great Depression still gripped America tightly, and voters strongly backed Roosevelt's New Deal and his allies in the Senate. The Democrats in the Senate gained a net of nine seats, giving them a supermajority—64 seats—two-thirds of the total 96 seats. This marked the first time since the Civil War that an incumbent president's party gained Senate seats during a midterm election. It was the Republican's worst year in decades. They lost 13 legislative seats. The voters elected a new House of 322 Democrats, 103 Republicans, and 10 Progressives or Farmer-Laborites. The dominating issue was the president himself. William Allen White commented, "He has been all but crowned by the people."[2]

As a judge, Mac distinguished himself by his availability and his judicial temperament. He was called "the kind of judge lawyers liked to practice before, even if the ruling went against them." It would not be long before judges would be precluded from private practice while serving as judges, but in the thirties, the judicial load was very light in rural counties. So Mac continued his private law practice while on the bench, just as he'd done while serving as county attorney. He took judging very seriously and very politically. He offered to travel to every county in Arizona and made friends with every judge on every court. He was the statewide expert on water law and knew more about the day-to-day problems faced by farmers and ranchers than any other judge. Ultimately, he presided as judge in trials in every Arizona county. He was reversed on appeal by the Arizona Supreme Court only three times in six years.[3] In his biography, Mac noted that he "enjoyed this work as much, or more than any other endeavor in his long career."

Some writers who later commented on Mac's six years as a trial judge in Arizona saw that period as one that focused largely on Arizona's historic search for water sources and farming stability. That certainly was the case, but it is equally clear that Mac took judging and law practice as important preludes to higher office. Running for office four times, winning twice and losing twice, were Mac's basic training for his long-hoped-for run for the U.S. Senate.

> I am frequently asked what part of my career I have enjoyed the most. I could hardly put any work above that of trial work while I was on the Superior Court bench. I was fortunate in that I was able to work hard until a decision was reached, and then put the case behind me. I have known judges who spent a lot of time trying to determine whether they had made a mistake after a decision was made. I was reversed only three times by our Supreme Court. The Superior Court in Arizona is a trial court, and at that time, it was the only court between the Justice of the Peace and the Supreme Court. Many interesting things happened in the trial of lawsuits. Sometimes I made decisions that were difficult to make during a trial, and would take consolation on having the Supreme Court to correct me if I made a mistake.[4]

Rural trial courts in Arizona were not full-time jobs and rarely involved complicated cases. But Mac had more than his share.

> One time, there was a black man brought before me on charges of burglary and arson. Apparently, he had thought if he burned the place down after burglarizing it, he would cover his tracks. The investigator for the insurance company and the sheriff's office had told him he would not receive more punishment for both burglary and arson than he would for a plea of guilty to burglary alone. So when he came before me, it was, of course my duty to advise him of his rights. That I did, and I asked him if he had an attorney and whether he had money to employ an attorney. I had to ask him a second time, and I changed

the word to 'lawyer.' He said, 'No, judge, your honor, I haven't any money to hire a lawyer.' I said, if you haven't a lawyer and you want a lawyer, it is my duty to appoint one for you. Do you want a lawyer?' He answered, 'Well, your honor, I don't see a lawyer could do any good. It looks to me like you could do me more good than a lawyer.' The prosecutor, Bill Truman, later Judge Truman, always said that I did.[5]

14

Mac and Edna, 1939

"EDNA E. SMITH, JUDGE MCFARLAND MARRY in Old Pueblo Ceremony" was the front-page headline in Florence on June 2, 1939. The quaint announcement was hardly news to anyone in Pinal County that summer. Mac grieved over his loss of Clare and their children in 1930 for just over a year. Then, given his enormous ambition, he returned to working long days in the courthouse and socializing in the evenings and on weekends. He became, what some called, Pinal County's most eligible bachelor for the next four years. He traveled widely and worked diligently. But a man of substance in those days could hardly stay a bachelor forever, especially if he had a higher office in his sights. He "frequently sought the company of Edna Smith," beginning in the summer of 1935.

Like Clare, Edna Eveland Smith was a teacher at Florence High School. Clare and Edna had been friends and shared a love of teaching. Edna—a widow according to some or a divorcee according to others—taught history and mathematics. She had earned her bachelor's degree at Parsons College in Iowa and went on to the University of Iowa, where she earned a master's degree in history. She taught in Denver, Colorado, for a time, then moved to Florence with her one-year-old daughter, Jewell, in 1930, the year Mac married Clare. Those who knew Mac and Edna socially were not in the least surprised about their eventual marriage, but many wondered about the length of the courtship. Smothering grief while learning to love again took a long time for Mac.

Edna, a lovely woman of high intellect and infinite patience, waited him out. Mac was said to have enjoyed his bachelorhood for a few years, but everyone was greatly relieved when Edna and Mac started a new life together at Mac's home "on tenth street," which the newspaper article said "was recently improved." The wedding photography accompanying the newspaper article depicts Mac facing the camera but leaning in toward Edna. He's wearing a light-tan suit and a brightly decorated necktie. Edna smiles modestly.

Edna was deeply involved in the Florence community, an active member of the Presbyterian church, and a strong supporter of many civic and social organizations. In her midthirties, she was said to be the perfect match for Florence's forty-year-old judge. The marriage in Tucson was a surprise to casual acquaintances, but not to Mac's or Edna's wide group of friends, colleagues, fellow teachers, and community leaders. It was a long ceremony, conducted at the home of one of Mac's best judicial friends, Pima County Judge William G. Hall. Mac was deep into his political campaign against Senator Ashurst and remarked that "he wanted to keep the ceremony from becoming a spectacle, as assuredly it would have been had we married at home in Florence."

Mac sought newspaper coverage wherever he could get it for political purposes, but he didn't want his marriage to be part of the political process. Still, some speculated he knew that bachelors rarely achieved high office, like the U.S. Senate. Mac's principal biographer put it this way: "Associates felt that Edna was 'one of the things that actually made Mac.' She was 'straight laced.' Mac was inclined to enjoy himself. But once they married, Mac settled down and really worked."

In his autobiography, Mac wrote, "I have been fortunate, however. I met and married another teacher, Edna Eveland Smith. Our family consisted of one daughter, Jewell. Edna was also talented and taught mathematics and history at Florence High School." These scant references to his family life in both his autobiography and in the longer 2004 biography by McMillan, give testament to Mac's longstanding dividing line between work and family. He could hardly stop talking politics, law, or farming, but he rarely talked about his family. Those who knew him best consistently honored his well-known dividing line.

Mac was a private man at home and a public man in court and the legislature. He worked just as hard to not expose his family in the press as he did to project his public views to anyone who willing to listen. He loved delivering speeches, shaking voters' hands, cutting political deals, and appearing in local and statewide newspapers. There would come a time when he made national and international news. But the dividing line for him was consistent. He thought the media ought to mind their manners when it came to personal matters.

15

Mac and Henry Fountain Ashurst, 1940

Henry Fountain Ashurst is famous, mostly, for what he said and how he said it. Known for his eloquence, most of what he said was admirable; some of it was genuinely humorous. But only one of his quotes strikes home in a book about the man who ousted him from the U.S. Senate. Ashurst famously said, "When I have to choose between voting for the people or the special interests, I always stick with the special interests. They remember. The people forget."

Mac remembered that quote, but never used it against the much-revered elder statesman. While Ashurst lost to Mac, it is the case that he was as worthy an adversary as Mac ever had. And from Mac's later acquired view, Ashurst was more worthy than the man who ultimately took Mac's Senate seat away from him in 1952: Barry Goldwater.

Ashurst was a legend in Arizona long before Mac came to Phoenix in 1919. His story resonated with Arizonans for three decades before Mac passed the bar. He was born in a sheep camp near Winnemucca, Nevada, in 1874, while his family was traveling westward in a covered wagon. They had given up their homestead in Missouri and planned to strike it rich in the gold fields in California. That part of Ashurst's story is lost in history, but his role in Arizona politics is well documented and widely known. His family moved to Williams, Arizona, in 1875. Two years later, they resettled to the Mormon Lake area south of Flagstaff. He went to grade and high school in Flagstaff, where he is still honored. Ashurst Hall at Northern Arizona University is named after him. When he turned eighty-five years old in 1959, he delivered the commencement address at Arizona State College in Flagstaff and received an honorary degree.

After high school, he attended college in Stockton, California, then went to the University of Michigan where he received a degree in legal studies. After his admission to the Arizona Bar Association in 1897, Ashurst, at twenty-three years old, returned to Williams and set up a one-man law office. Williams was small even by small-town standards. Its reported population in the 1890 census was 199. From there, Ashurst's march to office was a trajectory few Arizona politicians would ever match.

While it might be rural myth, there is a frequently told story about Ashurst's job as the turnkey at the Flagstaff jail when he was nineteen. He reportedly read William Blackstone's *Commentaries on the Laws of England* while studying law on the night shift in the prison. While not necessarily popular reading, the commentaries were influential eighteenth-century treatises on the common law of England, which was originally published between 1765 and 1769. The work focused grandly on the rights of persons, the rights of things, and the rights of private wrongs and public wrongs. Ashurst loved poetic, flowery language. In his later life, he frequently quoted Blackstone. Researchers at the turn of the twentieth century favored Blackstone because, even when the law was obscure, Blackstone sought to make it seem rational, just, and inevitable that things should be how they were. His book was famously used as the key in Benedict Arnold's book cipher, which he used to communicate secretly with his conspirator John André during their plot to betray the Continental Army during the American Revolution.

Like other Arizona territorial lawyers admitted to practice in 1897, Ashurst began his law practice without fanfare or the presence of another lawyer in town. He took cases for cash or barter. He kept only minimal records and rarely bothered with bar association matters. Williams was named after well-known trapper, scout, and mountain man "Old Bill Williams." In 1940, the phrase *old* would be applied again and again to Henry Ashurst.

In his day, Ashurst looked the exact opposite of contemporary portraits of Old Bill Williams. Williams, a man of the mountains, was always pictured as wild, unkempt, and ferocious, with a bulbous nose, a scraggly full beard, and homemade clothes, often made of animal skins. Ashurst favored frock coats, striped pants, winged collars, and highly polished shoes over silk stockings. He was usually photographed in a studio from an angle, rather than face on, and stood in formal pose, his right arm settled on the back of a chair and the left bent backward behind him. He was a bon vivant.

His first run for public office was his election to the Arizona Territorial House of Representatives in 1897. Reelected in 1899, he became the youngest speaker of the house in Arizona history. He moved to the Arizona Senate in 1902. When the legislature wasn't in session, he served as the district attorney of Coconino County from 1905 to 1908. He presided over Arizona's constitutional convention in 1911, where he positioned himself for the coveted appointment to the U.S. Senate when Arizona was granted statehood in 1912. He served in the U.S. Senate for twenty-nine years and was never seriously challenged until Mac took him on in 1940. Ashurst's oratorical skills defined him. Typical of his quotations was one he used in his successful 1936 campaign: "Praise underserved is scandal in disguise." He drew laughter from his self-deprecating sense of humor: "A speech is entertaining only when serenely detached from all information." Painfully true was his statement: "No man is fit to be a senator unless he is willing to surrender his political life for great principle." Perhaps the truest thing Ashurst ever said was a quip that surfaced in a *Time* magazine article about him: "I could throw 56-pound words clear across the Grand Canyon. Of course, I went into politics."

Ashurst, like all politicians, had his infuriating adversaries. One of his most troublesome rivals was a man named E. H. Duffield, a World War I veteran and a big fan of Mac's. Duffield wrote, and published, a booklet called *Six Letters to Senator Ashurst by an Ex-Soldier*. These letters were widely distributed at Mac's campaign rallies. The six letters are dated May 18, May 20, May 22, May 25, May 26, and July 2, 1940. No responses from Senator Ashurst were published, presumably because Ashurst wisely decided not to respond. Viewed strategically, all of the letters posed questions about Ashurst's position on the war raging in Europe while America "dithered." They are erudite, written in a knowledgeable first-person voice, and unquestionably aimed at Ashurst's isolationist views about European wars. The letters are long, engaging, and provocative.

In his first letter, Duffield referenced a May 18 radio program broadcast all over America.

> Dear Henry. This evening's radio brings the news that German military forces are within 70 miles of Paris. And the thought comes—how splendid would it be if, at the present moment, I could be one of two million or more American reinforcements available to the English and French military forces in France . . . Really, Henry, I have made an honest effort to get over there, and I find I impossible because of some neutrality feature of Congressional action of which Arizona's delegation has knowledge. It seems that all our ships are tied up in American ports and are forbidden to sail in restricted areas, due to fear that a German citizen named Hitler might take offense.

The balance of the May 18, 1940, letter clarifies Duffield's service "over there in 1918." He pesters Ashurst: "Really, Henry, how you could help me. Will you help me? The Boche is only 70 miles away." He questions Ashurst's patriotism: "Maybe I was all wrong when, on September 3, 1939 I took up the question with the War Department. Should I have taken up the question with you instead of them? I've known you since August 8, 1898. I know that you will not take the occurrence too seriously."

Duffield's next letter, written on May 20, 1940, ramps up the inquiry.

> I am wondering, Henry, about the Trojan Horse, sometimes called a Fifth Column, which it is said a German named Hitler has planted in those countries he is about to enter, some say conquer. Having heard, Henry, that the *Dies Committee* has discovered quite a few fellows among us, in low places, who could be classed as sabotagers, [sic] I am wondering if, by chance, the investigations by the *Dies Committee* are likely to uncover the fact that some in high places have reversed our policy of safety, as of Nov. 11, 1918, to our present position of unsafety. You have sat in Congress every day since Nov. 11, 1918. Maybe, Henry, I should not have mentioned your connection, your responsibility thusly . . . the Boche has advanced to Laon and San Quentin. I recall that there, at San Quentin, there was placed the astounding big, long-range German gun that

fired at 20-minute intervals upon Paris, 72 miles distant . . . Say, Henry do you anticipate that the French and English can, without our assistance defeat the Germans?

Two days later, Duffield penned an even longer and more narrowed attack to Ashurst.

Dear Henry: May I quote you from today's Paris news as carried in the Arizona Republic? 'Paul Reynaud, Premier, freely admitted the Boche has taken Amiens and Arras and were pouring through a 62-mile breach, thus taking the entire rear fortified system on that front.' Well, Henry that means that a million English, French, and Belgian solders are cut off and surrounded in Northern France . . . they may become prisoners of war . . . Do you recall, Henry, that in World War 1, Major Whittellsy (The Lost Battalion) likewise surrounded, failed to cut through his way back southward across that same 62-mile area occupied by hordes of Boche . . . What do you think, Henry, Hitler would do with so many English and French prisoners . . . ? I recall Henry, that a few years ago you visited England in your official capacity as a U.S. Senator from Arizona. You traveled under English sea supremacy. You went and returned leisurely at your own convenience as you willed it and without interference from any source. That, Henry, was possible because 21 allied nations had defeated Germany in the first world war—prevented them from taking the English and French navies and thereby becoming supreme on the seas since 1918 . . . Well Henry, it is hardly to be expected that a cowboy accustomed to life on the range could, even though he became a politician, learn much about sea power. You are running quite true to form as our national safety gets farther and farther out of hand . . . I have known you so long—41 years and 288 days. I know you will not take this seriously, or anything else, except getting votes seriously.

Duffield's May 25 letter was the longest of the six and clearly tied Ashurst to the editorial policy of the *Arizona Republic* on the eve of World War II.

Dear Henry, The Associated Press just carried the bad news that the Boche have just taken Calais, which is 22 miles distant from Dover, England. But the

Arizona Republic newspaper's editorial policy thus far has been, "We don't want to fight upon foreign lands." The situation recalls the last drive of the Boche in July 1918 when they took Chateau Thierry 22 miles distant from Paris, but were stopped by American Expeditionary Forces. Bullard wired Foch, 'No American soldier would understand why he was asked to fall back in such a situation as confronts me. I am attacking . . . Henry, there were two million of us over there then and not a single one of us today . . . Do you suppose Henry, that if there were two million of us there today, we could plug that 25-mile gap?

All of Duffield's letters peppered Ashurst about his political inaction vis-à-vis what Duffield saw as history repeating itself in one way—the Boche were taking over Europe—but not repeating itself since America—Ashurst's America—was looking the other way. He insisted that Ashurst look at Hitler's plan, which he outlined in his May 25 letter in some detail. He castigated Ashurst for his seeming agreement that the 1918 victory march was done by "suckers and warmongers." He accused Ashurst of "left-handed preaching of sedition, and destruction of patriotism." He tried to use Ashurst's style and voice. "Thus through your hands has vanished our safety and by your own action has the future battlefield upon American shores and acres been chosen."

Duffield's shortest but most damning letter was his May 26, 1940 missive.

Dear Henry, The Boche got across the River Meuse in Belgium and are now facing England from Calais because of Trojan Horse men in the French defense forces . . . in every country Hitler has taken, he had previously implanted his cooperatives in key places . . . In our country it was not necessary to implant cooperatives . . . They were already here. I believe you and your colleague, Carl Hayden, have sat every day since 1918, and John Murdock for almost four years during which we remained inactive while Hitler proceeded. The handwriting was on the wall for all to read. Our politicians ignored, so today you rush to spend billions for defense. Senators have a responsibility for people's safety.

His last letter, dated July 2, 1940, summarized his reasons for France's surrender to Germany—they did not have America's help when they needed it most. The results, Duffield tallied, are massive.

Results, utter defeat in a month-long blitzkrieg with casualties estimated at 1,500,000 killed, wounded, or missing. A stunned nation only now beginning to realize what happened, a stunned leadership groping toward the future . . . Well, Henry, this brings to mind what I saw in Paris on December 13, 1918.

Duffield wrote several paragraphs recalling his experience and the grandeur of the city's decorations, Woodrow Wilson's presence, the silent muzzles of the German field pieces, and how safe and wonderful France looked because America came to her aid. He chastised Ashurst since

> we elected you and returned you again and again for twenty-one years but now our safety is no longer ours—it has vanished, utterly gone. It is said, Henry, that you are asking for re-election—for the trust and support of the people of Arizona. Well, professional politicians neglected the defense of France and so have our professional politicians neglected ours. Both guilty as Germany proceeds from Austria, thence through several other countries to England, and then where? And you ask for re-election! Sincerely, E. H. Duffield.

Duffield's six letters were collected and put into booklet form. The booklets were passed out at scores of rallies and read by thousands of Arizona voters. The booklets today are among the archived papers of a great many politicians running for election in 1940. There would be much more to come when Mac announced his candidacy against Henry Fountain Ashurst.

16

Mac's Primary Campaign Against Henry Fountain Ashurst, 1940

No one in Arizona was better prepared to take on a political icon like Henry Fountain Ashurst than Mac was in the summer of 1940. Ashurst's only formal legal education was one year at Michigan Law in 1903. Mac mounted an attack based on the many years he'd spent at three universities, from which he earned four degrees. Ashurst's advantage could have been his strong legislative record. As history would later record, Ashurst squandered that advantage by not even bothering to return to Arizona from his Washington, DC, home to campaign in the 1940 primary campaign.

Mac's decision to run for the Senate took more than a year of deliberation, consultation, and risk assessment. And that was just the *immediate* decision to run. Once made, Mac and his small group of planners took another month to create a timetable and a priority list. In his masterful political biography, McMillan outlined the call as a nine-year-long series of decisions beginning with how to overcome the loss of his first family at age thirty-six and culminating in the start of a new family at age forty-six. McMillan titled this period of Mac's life the "Road to the Senate: 1931–1940."

Mac "struggled to pick up the pieces of his life, and leave the tragedy behind; not an immediately achievable task."[1]

Mac's 1979 autobiography confirms the end result while giving scant notice to the tragedy and speaking only in a nuanced voice, decades later.

> Anyone with ambitions for a political career should stop occasionally, look ahead, and determine what the next step should be. Should you quit, stay on in your present job, or should you aspire to another, perhaps higher office? The answer to this manifold question is usually personal to the individual and family; however, one is usually guided by lifetime ambitions. In this regard, I do not claim to be different from the majority of those running for office. Ambitions frequently harken back to boyhood days. I well remember the time on the prairie farm when we labored long hours to get ahead. I had dreams of an education. I had always looked upon law and political life as honorable achievements.[2]

That Mac always aspired to political office is evident in his own words, as was his decisional premise: "Those of us who aspire to political office frequently jump to conclusions without fair appraisal. A person should realize that there are always a few people who will offer words of encouragement without foundation for the opinion."[3]

Equally evident is the ultimate goal, the one that mattered most in his thirties, but would be encapsulated in his fifties and sixties:

> The position I really wanted then was United States Senator from Arizona. Senator Henry Ashurst had held the office for twenty-eight years, and was regarded by many as unbeatable. My friends asked me how I expected to beat a man like Senator Ashurst. I told them I was going to slip up on him—that I would lay a foundation which would be difficult for him to overcome at the last minute.

Henry Fountain Ashurst had built a formidable reputation in the U.S. Senate over several decades. He was a hard-riding former sheriff from Coconino County in the territorial nineteenth century. In his twenty-eighth year in the state senate in 1940, he was ranked second in seniority and chaired the powerful judiciary committee. They called him the "silver-tongued orator of the Senate." There was much to admire and no small number of miscues to take advantage of. *Time* magazine called him the "silver-tongued sunbeam" in August 1939.[4] Among other sobriquets, he was called the "dean of inconsistency, and five-syllable Henry."[5]

Mac was fond of telling the story about how he beat the silver-tongued orator: "One good friend from Prescott asked me how I expected to be elected to the Senate 'from a little old town like Florence.' I told him that the people of Phoenix and the people of Tucson were jealous of each other, and feelings sometimes played a part in campaigns. But that neither would be jealous of someone running for office from Florence."[6]

The big day for Mac finally came on April 26, 1940; he announced his candidacy.

"Arizona needs another senator who is interested primarily in Arizona."

The message was clear. Senator Carl Hayden and Judge Ernest McFarland truly cared about Arizona. Ashurst cared about Washington, DC.

Six weeks later, on June 15, 1940, Ashurst rose in the Senate and announced his candidacy for re-election. He said he was opposed by "able and worthy opponents" and expressed a desire to return to his home state. However, he concluded that he would be unworthy of his position if he did so during the stressful times the nation was facing. Ashurst was a familiar name everywhere. Mac was termed by Ashurst supporters as "merely a country judge in one of Arizona's least important counties." Ashurst's wife had died the previous year, and the family had spent little time in Arizona. He felt himself invulnerable to the challenge of an obscure opponent and devised no specific strategy for the election contest.

Ashurst did not visit Arizona during the primary campaign. Mac went to thirty-six Arizona cities and towns; he visited every county, every courthouse, and he never missed a rodeo, dance hall, or a newspaper office. Mac followed a trail left by his mentor, Governor George P. Hunt. He slowly and quietly amassed a large circle of friends, fellow judges, lawyers, newspapermen, farmers, and ranchers. He had held court and tried cases before juries in every county in the three years before the 1940 primary campaign was announced, and Mac opened his campaign in Casa Grande, not Florence, in his old law office.

His nine-point attack was tightly focused and based on conversations with hundreds of Arizonans in 1939. He clearly knew Arizona's mind-set.

First, America must create a strong national defense and ready itself for the horror that was about to engulf Europe. Second, America must send appropriate aid to Great Britain. Third, we must take aggressive action against fifth columnists. Fourth, we must protect tariffs, especially in the mining industries. Fifth, end the federal government's involvement in stock and range management. Sixth, find ways to preserve for American markets our domestic labor and industry. Seventh, provide federal aid for agriculture, especially Arizona cotton. Eighth, fully develop the water in the Colorado River for use in Arizona. Ninth, elect a senator who knows and lives in Arizona, not one who only knows Washington, DC, and spends all his time there.[7]

As it turned out, Mac's final campaign bullet was one of his best. Ashurst, perhaps unknowingly, exacerbated the issue. In the spring of 1940, the Senate majority leader, Alben Barkley proposed a recess so senators could go home for the summer start of the primary campaign. Ashurst rose to denounce such a policy, saying, "Those who vote to go home should be kept there . . . for the remainder of their career."[8] Ashurst threatened delay of pending legislation to keep Congress in session all summer before election. Mac responded locally and frequently. In just three months, Mac wore down Ashurst's credibility and his in-absentia campaign pressed only by surrogates, not the silver-tongued orator himself.

Mac never tried to speak in Ashurst's flowery oratorical flourishes. Mac was who he said he was—a homespun lawyer and a rural county judge. He projected vast, certain knowledge of national issues while personifying grassroots issues with common-sense explanations. He didn't speak above or down to his Arizona audiences. He informed them in ways no one before him had ever tried to do. One thing Mac insisted on was the avoidance of what, today, is called *negative campaigning*. He was never overly critical of his opponent. He kept some items about Ashurst under wraps. Mac had meticulously researched Ashurst's finances and patronage. Beginning in May 1940, Mac talked to Washington connections, who looked into Ashurst's property taxes and valued the salaries of Ashurst's office staff. They told Mac that Ashurst was entitled, as head of the judiciary committee, to employ one secretary and three clerks. But he employed only two people, using his wife's and another's name to draw the complete four salaries.

As McMillan pointed out, "There were other similar misdeeds."[9] The salary of an Ashurst staff employee from Mesa was surreptitiously put toward an automobile, which had been used for at least one transcontinental trip for Ashurst and his wife. A domestic worker in the Ashurst home drew government salary, and except for a single office assistant doorkeeper, the senator had employed no one from Arizona. But Mac did not want to embarrass Ashurst, and he avoided disclosing any of his financial discoveries during the campaign.

His years as a working lawyer and his time on the trial bench gave Mac a natural way of articulating differences of commitment between opposing sides in a lawsuit. He used that core tactic against Ashurst; Ashurst was frequently inconsistent because he played the tune of the day rather than the song of a long campaign. Mac used Ashurst's record of inconsistency against him, which was a trait Ashurst had always regarded as a positive attribute: "My faults are obvious . . . I suffer from *cocoethes loquendi*, a mania or itch for talking . . . but there never has been super-added to these vices of mine the withering embalming vice of consistency." That voice seemed to play well in the salons of Washington but had little resonance on Arizona's campaign trails.

Mac quickly established Ashurst's inconsistencies. He had shifted from dry to wet on the topic of prohibition. He moved from low to high on tariff support. On cotton subsidy, Ashurst expressed confusion because the senators on whom he usually depended were in dispute. He said, "I presume I must resort to the rather unpleasant idea of making up my own mind." On silver, Ashurst said, "Nothing has ever been able to make a breach in the wall that surrounds and protects the reservoir of ignorance I possess on the money question." Concerning his tariff shift, Ashurst echoed Arron Burr, whom he revered, saying, "I do not rise to exclaim or disclaim anything. My policy in life has been never to explain because if today one explains, tomorrow he will be explaining the explanation."[10]

Mac was consistently both a "wet" and a high tariff man. He was a cotton farmer himself. He may have erred occasionally, but he was never in doubt, and always quick to decide.

One of the most dominant themes in the summer of 1940 was then called the Townsend Plan, a social security plan for elderly citizens. Mac stressed

Ashurst's equivocation from opposition to late support for the plan and emphasized the 1937 Supreme Court fight over the issue. There, Ashurst had initially stood against Roosevelt's court packing idea. Then, as judiciary committee chair, he worked hard to push the plan through before ultimately voting with the majority against Roosevelt's proposal. Mac sharply articulated each deviation.[11]

At home, Mac said Ashurst acted too slowly on the most important issue in the state—water. Although it took twenty-eight years, Ashurst seemed to only have recently recommended a survey to determine the feasibility of bringing Colorado River water to central Arizona.

Mac questioned the depth of Ashurst's commitment to defense and preparedness. While Ashurst knew the state of European warfare in 1939 and early 1940, he said little about it in Arizona. Mac developed a strategic outlook based on national press coverage. While the outbreak of "the European war" initiated many preparedness measures, the sequence of events in the late summer and fall of 1939 was thought by many to lessen the imminence of a military threat to the United States and other portions of the Western Hemisphere. Canada's declaration of war against Germany in September 1939 put the northeastern front of the hemisphere on the alert. After Germany's quick triumph over Poland, the European war settled into a lull that remained unbroken until April 1940. Pending a showdown between Germany and Anglo-French military power, many thought there was little threat to the Americas. Most Americans in the summer of 1940 were sympathetic to Great Britain and France, but most wanted to avoid direct participation in another European war. Roosevelt and his advisers had the same goal, seeing no serious threat to the Western Hemisphere that could arise unless the British and French were pushed to the brink of defeat. In that event, the United States would face the grim choice of supporting Great Britain and France by vastly increasing American naval power. Mac was an early adopter of the need for preparedness and defense. Ashurst was not.

Mac caught Ashurst somewhat unawares by introducing a fresh policy issue into the campaign when the first peacetime conscription bill stood before the Senate having passed in the House. The Phoenix Junior Chamber of Commerce urged both candidates to support conscription. Ashurst did not, and Mac did, saying the issue was "above politics" and would speed up national preparedness and increase the probability of avoiding war.

Ashurst telegrammed the chamber: "With true respect and esteem for all, I should be lacking in candor and deficient in frankness if I failed to say that I could not vote for this bill." Ashurst bolstered his position on the illusion of American strength, the pervasive and negative influence of European militarism, and the threat of a peacetime draft becoming a permanent fixture on the domestic front. When the bill passed, Mac once again appeared more in line with Roosevelt and public opinion.

Mac questioned Ashurst's source for campaign funding by pointing out that in 1934, the senator received large contributions from eastern bankers, including $1,000 from Bernard Branch. Mac clarified that he deplored eastern colonialism of the West and disclaimed any connections to eastern interests. Mac spent $12,000 out of his own pocket for campaigning and accepted only in-state contributions. But this point was moot because, in 1940, Ashurst spent only $2,072.66 on campaigning, including $412 of his own money.[12]

Besides Mac and Ashurst, three outlier candidates ran in the Democratic primary that summer. Stockton Henderson, Edwin Karz, and Robert Miller identified themselves as candidates for the position. Henderson was a Phoenix lawyer widely regarded as a stalking horse for Ashurst. Edwin Karz, also a Phoenix lawyer, and Robert Miller, a pharmacist, were there only to split up Mac's votes. Mac made short work of the outliers. His campaign mailed thousands of copies of a June 5, 1940, editorial from *The Messenger*, titled "Political Perfidy." That newspaper dismissed Miller as "utterly unequipped by training or experience." Karz dismissed himself, withdrawing from the race and endorsed Mac. Stockton was linked to a probable repetition of Ashurst's 1934 ticket-splitting tactics. The newspaper characterized him as a "man of straw," involved in a sham effort to split the anti-Ashurst vote. Stockton reported no personal expenditures for his campaign. Mac paid little personal attention to any of them; he focused entirely on Ashurst.[13]

Stockton made a speech on August 30, 1940, in Tucson proclaiming Mac was "not eligible to try for the office." He filed suit against Mac's eligibility in Maricopa County, basing his case on the Arizona Constitution, which stated that "judges of the Supreme Court and judges of the superior court shall not be eligible to any office or public employment during the term for which they have been elected." Mac was in the middle of his second term as Pinal County's superior judge; his term was scheduled to expire January 1, 1943.[14]

Mac treated the suit as groundless and relied on the U.S. Constitution, which stated, "Each house shall be the judge of the elections, returns, and qualifications of its own members."

The Arizona Supreme Court, led by Chief Justice Arthur T. LaPrade unanimously agreed, stating the state constitution provision could be applied only to offices created by the Arizona Constitution and therefore could not apply to posts set up in the U.S. Constitution.[15] Stockton's weak court filing gave Mac an unintended boost. It gathered Mac's supporters into a tighter knit community, and he won the primary in a landslide. Mac took 10 of the 14 counties, including Pinal, by a 12-to-1 margin. He won Maricopa and Pima by 35,243 to 17,748. Ashurst barely won his home base of Flagstaff–Prescott.

After the primary, both candidates reflected positively on the election results. Ashurst was magnanimous in defeat and Mac generous in victory. Mac and Ashurst exchanged telegrams, Ashurst offering "heartiest congratulations" and stating he would "come to campaign joyously for you and the entire state ticket." Mac wired back, "Most sincere thanks for your very kind wire. It represents the highest type of sportsmanship." Stockton, embittered, wrote a different telegram: "Being a Democrat, I shall support all the nominees of my party, notwithstanding the false charges that I was Senator Ashurst's stooge and that he financed my campaign made by you, and your associates throughout the state, knowingly and maliciously with full knowledge of their falsity, and notwithstanding your deliberate and premeditated assignation of my character."[16]

17

Mac's Retail Politics, 1940

In today's political world, politics *is* mass marketing. Even local races are Twitter-driven, poster-sized, and managed by professionals. In twenty-first-century electioneering, only wholesale politics works, and the focus is always on swaying groups rather than individuals. But in Mac's 1940 run for national office, politicking was pure retail—one vote at a time. Mac was the one pressing the flesh, not just his surrogates. He wrote the notes by hand. He often took them to the post office for mailing. He drove his own car—often on dirt roads, and wearing out shoe leather, in bars, barber shops, churches, rodeo grounds, camp sites, and big city parks. Now those quaint political customs are relegated to buggy-whip status. All of that has been replaced by pressing keyboards and clicking online *donate-now* buttons. Candidates don't work rooms anymore, they work platforms and airport lounges. Conveying the sincerity of your message depends on attractive, well-designed logos, clever handles, biting hashtags, and leaking documents—real or fake. Little thought is given now about how the candidate feels on specific topics, much less how the voter takes in air.

Even so, the 1930s had its political upgrades. Franklin Delano Roosevelt had his "brain trust": men much concerned with economic conditions and the dilemmas of the times. His inner circle was well versed in political theory

Mac leading the Florence Parada, ca. 1940.

and economic philosophy. They felt unhampered by traditional ideas. The Democrats were largely focused on decisions that would promote the general welfare and governmental failures to protect the public interest. The Republicans abhorred government interference and insisted the country would right itself if it was just left alone. Witticisms like the "eight-hundred-pound gorilla in the room" hadn't yet been invented, but war in Europe, and a stagnant economy, were the cultural equivalent.

Mac was as good at retail politics as any candidate Arizona had ever seen. His brain trust was made up mostly of judges, lawyers, farmers, and stockmen from every county in the state. With their help, Mac made daily eye-to-eye contact with voters, wrote real letters on stiff paper with individually licked postage stamps, and spoke at rallies that were always dual-purposed: get Mac in front of crowds and mingling with local leaders. Wherever he went, he was up close, physically in touch, and always listening carefully. He was as sincere as a high school valedictorian and as candid as a mirror.

Style in 1930s politics could be aggressive. Sometimes personal attacks worked, particularly on the Republican side of the aisle. But Mac was never negative, in person or in print, and was never known to say anything explicitly designed to tarnish his opponent's reputation. This gave Mac an advantage because he was not nearly as well known as Ashurst. By shaking hands and sharing meals, hot dogs, Coca-Cola, popcorn, and ice cream, voters got to know him personally. In stark contrast, Ashurst voters in Arizona mostly knew him as a man more than a little past his prime and very much flattered with his own image. He often seemed uncomfortable, distracted, bored, or put off. But his biggest political sin was his absence; Mac had much of the field to himself. Complete strangers, once exposed to Mac's charm and local "feel," were easily swayed in his favor. Mac was "one of them—in every town." He made sure everyone saw him driving his own car and paying for his own coffee and ice cream. In every town, he *visited* with people rather than just speaking from a dais. Even so, it was not just his personal presence that attracted voters. His personal letters cemented his position and garnered him votes by the thousands.

For today's lawyers and judges, the relationship between Mac, his fellow judges, and his political campaign would have been difficult to understand. Judges then, like today, were subject to canons of ethics. Judicial canons were said to "speak for themselves and require no extended comment or interpretation." Canon 28, titled *Partisan Politics*, as amended in 1933, condemned all participation in political campaigns and discussions, including speeches, endorsement of candidates, and contributions. However, there was an exception. Where it was necessary for judges to be nominated and elected as candidates of a political party, nothing "contained herein shall prevent the judge from attending or speaking at political gatherings, or from making contributions to campaign funds of the party that has nominated him and seeks his election or reelection." That canon focused on judicial campaigns, rather than nonjudicial offices. In any event, there was no shortage of lawyer or judicial involvement in Mac's campaign against a fellow lawyer in both his primary and general election runs for the U.S. Senate in 1940.

The Lawyer Letters

Mac's 1940 campaign letters are archived at the Polly Rosenbaum Archives and History Building in Phoenix. While there is no actual count or alphabetical list of the letters, they number in the tens of thousands, dutifully filed in scores of cardboard boxes—it would take weeks to read them all. The letters and related documents reflect Mac's political life starting with his admission to the Arizona Bar Association in 1921 and ending with his retirement from the Arizona Supreme Court in 1971. The bulk of the collection relates to his election to and service in the U.S. Senate from 1940 to 1952. It's no surprise that several thousand letters were to or from lawyers and judges throughout Arizona and other states. The following small sample is a glimpse into how Mac's relationship with judges, lawyers, sheriffs, and police officers advanced both the rule of law *and* Mac's political career.

Martin Herlick, a Phoenix lawyer, wrote to Mac on August 29, 1940, and reported that several of his close friends were doing all they could for his campaign: "I have some of your literature in my law office at 815 West Adams Street. Feel welcome to drop in if over this way, any time."

Mac exchanged correspondence with Frank Gold, a lawyer from Flagstaff: "I am somewhat dependent upon friends like yourself to assist me in my campaign. I appreciated your telling me you were going to help me for I know you are a man of influence."

A. G. Netherlin, attorney-at-law from Ajo, Arizona, asked Mac to "send me some of your cards. I have been out for some time. Mr. Albert I. Long wants to pass some of them too. So far as I can tell things seem to be all right here for you."

Mac wrote back to Elmer Graham, a Phoenix lawyer, and thanked him for the information about his campaign and for his "interest in my welfare."

John P. Clark was the Navajo County Superior Court judge in Holbrook and carried petitions in that county for Mac. He told Mac in a July 19, 1940, letter that Judge Udall (then on the Arizona Supreme Court) "is helping with petitions but they need more."

Judge Henry C. Kelly presided over the Yuma County Superior Court. He wrote to Mac on July 5, 1940, asking for copies of "good campaign articles" and offering helpful suggestions about campaigning. He suggested Mac tailor some of his speeches to the many Oklahoma and Texas folks now making Arizona their home. "You can capitalize on that very effectively by a discrete reference to your place of birth. We can help you reach our population over local radio here." He said "more newspaper publicity is available if you can arrange to come down here again."

Mac made no bones about Judge Kelly's help: "I realize this is a big state and with a small amount of money to run on, it is hard; however, with friends like yourself boosting for me I do not how I can fail. I appreciate your support more than I can express in a letter."

The 1920s and 1930s spawned the formation of clubs of all kinds throughout the western states. In what was probably not intended as a double-entendre, the name *Active 20–30* was first chartered in 1924 in Washington State by a group of young men, aged 20 to 39, to secure a more active part in the affairs of their hometowns. Between 1924 and 1940, charters were granted to 260 clubs with more than 5,000 members. About 65 percent of those young men would serve in World War II, including a young lawyer from Phoenix named J. A. Riggins. Known as Ted by every lawyer in Phoenix, Riggins was the president of the Phoenix Active 20–30 club when Mac announced his intention to run for the U.S. Senate. He wrote to Mac on July 17, 1940, and offered Mac his personal support and the support from the entire membership of the club. He put the matter in both funny and serious terms.

> I recently gave the members an examination to find out what they knew about their state, and country. One of the questions sought a cross-section opinion

that you will find interesting. I asked our members, 'Who is the senior US Senior from Arizona and for what is he noted? The following answers were received: "Ashurst, for what little he does for Arizona; Ashurst; flowery speech and not getting much done; Ashurst; bullshit; Ashurst; Sesquepedalian words; Ashurst; bombastic oratory and not a damn thing; Ashurst; speeches in which he says nothing."

Mr. Riggins cautioned Mac. "If you should by chance show this list to anyone, I shall of course appreciate you're not mentioning then the name of the club or my name in connection with it. Wishing you every success in the campaign and hoping that I may be of some help, I remain, very truly yours, Ted Riggins."

The irony in this exchange will not be obvious to most readers; Riggins was a big help in both the primary campaign against Ashurst and in the general campaign against Irving A. Jennings. After Jennings lost to Mac, he invited Riggins to join his law firm, then known as Jennings & Strouss. It eventually became the state's largest firm.[1]

The 1111 Club in Phoenix, run by another up-and-coming lawyer, Lou Miller, had a block heading on the letter he sent to Mac on September 5, 1940: "ELEVEN HUNDRED ELEVEN VOTES FOR GOOD GOVERNMENT IN ARIZONA." The club had had two factions: the "rainy-day club" and the "silent-vote club." They were "not interested in political booty, but will go out and vote if they feel their vote will help the state." They secured and sent to Mac a copy of a petition they had circulated securing the signatures of "one thousand, one hundred, and eleven voters to vote for Mac on September 10th."

Mac wrote back the next day.

Words cannot express my appreciation for your letter and the 1111 Club Pledge. Be assured it will remain in my confidential file. I am in such a hurry these last few days, that, even if I were as glib-tongued as our Henry, I hardly have time to say hello to my wife. I do know, however, that no man can be elected to high office in this state without unselfish and non-political support such as is given me by your group. Again, thank you; thank you! Sincerely, Mac.

Mohave County's most prominent lawyer at the time of the 1940 U.S. Senate campaign was Frank X. Gordon. He told Mac in his June 5, 1940, letter he had secured "260 signatures" on a petition for Mac. He said he had talked to "Judge Faulkner and he will get something for you." In his July 9 letter to Mac, he reported that he had put up campaign posters in Kingman and was doing the "best I can for you." He sent Mac a long list of other prominent citizens he had contacted on Mac's behalf. Mac received dozens of letters from men who didn't know him, but said they'd been contacted by Frank Gordon and urged to vote for him. Mac answered every one, acknowledging the significant help Gordon was to his campaign. He received three more completed petitions from Mr. Gordon on July 22. The support and friendship would turn out to last three decades.

Somerton lawyer R. H. Theilmann was another big supporter who voted and campaigned for Mac. While he knew Mac, his political support was mostly vested in opposing Ashurst. He made that clear in his April 28, 1940, letter to Mac.

> You and I can be considered old acquaintances—we officially met many times in your court, and on the road. I want to vote for a senator vs. Ashurst. Hence this letter. My man must positively be against the Santa Fe Colorado River compact in any form whatsoever. I count it as important as any nullification, or secession. Your position against that compact must be ironclad. It involves the life of the state.

Mac wrote back on May 10: "Your letter of a few days ago is at hand. I note you are interested in the fight for our rights in the Colorado River. You of course know that I made talks against the ratification of the Santa Fe River compact several years ago."

A month later, on June 10, Theilmann wrote back: "It is not often that a chance arises like the present. This is the end of the career of Henry F. Ashurst. I saw the situation quite a few years ago and this is the first real hit that has been given him. It is time Arizonans showed some sense! The subject is too large for one letter. Have your advisers put their heads together and evolve a quick 'Blitzkrieg' plan, and hit the ball."

The Arizona Voters

Perhaps the best example among the thousands of Mac's "retail" voters was a woman named Viola Gray. Gray lived on the Eureka Ranch near Bonita, Arizona. They exchanged several letters and had two in-person meetings during the campaign. Mac's May 22, 1940, letter to her was the first in a summer-long exchange between them.

> Dear Mrs. Gray, I am in receipt of a letter from your father in which he states that you expressed a desire to assist me in my campaign in Wilcox. I am grateful to you for your interest and inasmuch as Mr. Boone stated that you were willing to circulate some of my petitions, I am enclosing some herewith.

She wrote back on June 15, following up on an earlier personal meeting:

> Enclosed are three of the petitions. Do I have time to finish the other one? We live 48 miles from Wilcox now on the Eureka Ranch and only go to town once a week. But if I have a few more weeks, I'll finish all the petitions. Wilcox seems to be rather strong for Ashurst, but maybe we can change them. Mr. Beverly, the mayor is strong for you; also the ex-mayor, Mr. Swanner. The freight agent there, I've forgotten his name, is a strong Ashurst man. I hope these names I'm sending you will help you. I'll keep talking and telling them that McFarland must be our next Senator. Sincerely, Viola M. Gray.

On June 24, Mac wrote back:

> I greatly appreciate the good work you have done in Wilcox and thank you for the petitions you have filed. I will be making a trip to Wilcox soon. A vote for Arizona league has been organized in my behalf. My friends are contacting their acquaintances and I expect to be rather well known there soon. Thanking you again for your help and assuring you that I will welcome any suggestions of information you have in the future, I am, Sincerely Yours, Ernest W. McFarland.

Mrs. Gray answered on July 1. "I just finished reading a circular Dad sent me. Could you send me some of those circulars by return mail, as I expect to spend the weekend in Wilcox? I'll be in Patagonia—40 miles away—on a ranch. There are about 40 cowboys and other employees. I can help you with them. There are forty cowboys on our ranch and I can assure you they will cast their votes for you."

Mac wrote back on July 3 and effusively thanked her. Gray answered on August 23 and reported her efforts:

> I have called on the 76 Ranch. Mrs. Webb is a very earnest booster of yours. Everyone at the A.J. Mills Ranch, also the DeBoise Ranch will vote for you. Part of the bunch at the Brookerson Ranch are supporters of yours now—the others are Ashurst's. Maybe between now and voting time, I can win them over. There are five other big ranches I want to get to soon and if you think of anyone else out this way for me to call on, let me know. Tomorrow we go to Safford. Oh yes, the Carters that live just outside of Wilcox are pulling teeth and toe nail for you since you came to Wilcox and shook hands with them. In fact, those handshakes changed several of them. Yours truly, Viola M. Gray.

Mac carried Cochise County by a comfortable margin thanks to his attention to the small details of running for national office and his ability to communicate with voters like Gray.

In addition to his heavy reliance on the U.S. Postal Service, Mac also engaged, as he put it, "eyeball to eyeball, with every active Democratic group, civic, or social club, man, or women I meet on the street."

Mac knew how closely ranching and farming families were connected to hunting and fishing. Hundreds of "form" letters went out over his signature with a plain addressee: "Dear Fellow Sportsman." These letters emphasized the "proper protection of our game and fish." He reminded his voters,

> The State Fish and Game Commission sold licenses to over 30,000 sportsmen and women. As the wonders of bass fishing at Lake Mead, Parker Dam and other spots gets voiced around, more and more people from other states are going to make use of our ever-improving highway system to come to Arizona

for their fishing and hunting. Many tens of thousands of dollars are spent in this manner each year, and the total can be increased materially by a careful program. If elected to the United States Senate, I propose to make the care and preservation of our game and fish one of my major concerns. My plan includes (1) a federal bass hatchery for Southern Arizona to supplement the small amount we now have at Papago Park, near Phoenix; (2) a federal trout hatchery in some suitable place in the northern portion of our state; (3) an increased appropriation to the U.S. Biological Survey for the purpose of cutting across the appalling losses credited to predatory killers; (4) a proper and just proportion of the Pittman-Robbinson funds to be allocated to Arizona to develop game reserves; (5) to secure an appropriation for the development of a recreational area at Parker Dam and for the Boulder Dam use of our own citizens and winter visitors. I am hoping you will find this letter of interest and take it for what it really is—a sincere program intelligently drawn up in your interest. Your support of this program will be deeply appreciated.

While this letter was directed to Arizona's sportsmen and women, Mac knew how critical the Hoover Dam, which formed Lake Mead, was for many reasons other than fishing. Once known as Boulder Dam, it was constructed between 1931 and 1936. Roosevelt dedicated it on September 30, 1935. The dam's construction was a massive effort involving thousands of workers and costing more than one hundred lives. It became America's largest reservoir and provided power for public and private utilities in Arizona, California, and Nevada. It was widely considered a prime source of irrigation water downstream in Arizona and California because it backed up the Colorado River. He consistently praised and supported legislation focused on getting Arizona its fair share of that water.

Mac's campaign team organized "McFarland for U.S. Senator" clubs all over the state. His team assured him that "nearly 100% of the voters in Pinal County favored you over Henry Ashurst in the primary campaign." This fact was widely distributed in letters, pamphlets, and posters in all other counties. The campaign logo, *For Real Representation, Elect Ernest W. McFarland, Democrat—U.S. Senator*, was mimeographed onto tens of thousands of penny postcards.

Mac's judicial secretary was also his law office secretary. She typed and sent thousands of letters and tens of thousands of handwritten postcards from her office at the Pinal County courthouse. One of them, to a Tucson man, L. V. Corkum, illustrates how effective this piece of retail politicking was.

> I am enclosing one of my postcards so you can see what they are like. The space beneath the printed message up in the corner is for personal hand-written messages and the signature of the sender. They are cheap and effective . . . If you could use any, or would care to contact any of your friends in the Judge's behalf by using these cards, we would be happy to furnish you with as many as you want. I do not wish to burden you, but I am so enthusiastic and anxious for the Judge to win that I suggest this way in which people who want to do so can help him . . . If this appears to be a too lengthy letter, it is only because I have been the Judge's secretary for a long time and have had the opportunity of learning what a fine person he is and I want everyone in the State of Arizona to know that we are fortunate in having man of the Judge's caliber in the race.

The letter was signed, "Very truly yours, Secty."

Mac was very involved in education issues—as both Pinal County attorney, and Pinal County judge. Those contacts were helpful in his political campaigns. The Pinal County school superintendent, John J. Bugg, sent out many letters to other officials and local parents of students in his system. Typical of those letters was one he wrote to W. T. Machan on August 15, 1940.

> I should like to submit to you the candidacy of Judge E. W. McFarland for the United States Senate. It has been my pleasure to know the Judge for fifteen years and can authentically vouch for his ability to serve Arizona as a senator in such a way that its citizens will be thoroughly pleased. Judge McFarland's education, training and general ability to understand the problems that are facing the state relative to the mines, livestock and other industries fit him for this responsible position in such a way that Arizona will benefit by his election. He is acquainted with Arizona and her needs better than any man I know; is respected throughout the state and can secure the cooperation of

leaders in solving the problems incident to our southwest. Please investigate this man. I am sure it will result in your active support of his campaign in the forthcoming election.

This letter, like many others he wrote, was printed on letterhead stationary from the Pinal Department of Education and signed John J. Bugg, County School Superintendent. By way of example how powerful these letters were, one recipient of the letter wrote back.

> Dear John, I am definitely ashamed of Ashurst. Two votes here for McFarland. Sincerely, Mack.

A prominent assayer and chemist from Kingman wrote a September 4 letter to Mac reporting his situation.

> Well, dear friend Mac, Mohave County is in the bag for you. I will say at the very least that it will be five or six to one. I've been to all the mining camps all over the county. Put your cards out everywhere. You have got it in the bag but do not let up. I am going to watch here and see if they try and pull anything. If there is anything else I can do for you up here, you know I am at your service anytime or anything you want done. A. V. Stevenson.

Jack Murphy was Mac's campaign chairman during his term as assistant attorney general for Arizona. He had many friends and colleagues checking Ashurst's campaign. George Bideaux was the editor of the *Southwest Veteran* in Tucson. Bideaux wrote to Murphy on September 8, just two days before the votes were cast in the Arizona Democratic primary election.

> Jack, here are a few clippings. The Ashurst outfit got busy this weekend and put on a little blitzkrieg, but I think most people have already made up their minds to support the Judge. I want to compliment you on the way you have handled the campaign. You came in at just the right time, and it looks like a sure victory. When I consented to help the Judge down here early in the campaign, it looked like an almost hopeless effort. The picture is different now.

George W. Tewksbury shows up in several of Mac's correspondence files. He was the executive secretary of the Arizona Spanish-American Progressive Association. He wrote to Mac on August 29.

> Dear Sir, At a recent meeting of this organization, for the purpose of choosing the candidate's names that we are going to endorse, your name was placed before us by Mr. J. W. Wentworth, Clerk of the Superior Court for Gila County. Due to the very good talk he made in your behalf, the vote of endorsement went to you. That means that as members we will do all in our power in your behalf.

That letter went on at some length to describe how they would help Mac. They ran a full-page ad, in Spanish, addressed to Latin American voters. They would distribute three thousand handbills all over Gila County and would "reach every Latin-American home in Gila County." They did all of this "at a large cost for our organization." All they asked in return was that "if the candidate wishes to donate something to help us pay the costs, we will gratefully appreciate it." A handwritten postscript on the bottom of the latter said, "No other U.S. Senate candidate has or will be contacted. This is the only officially recognized Spanish Political Organization in Gila County."

A handwritten note on the letter suggests that Mac's campaign made a ten-dollar donation.

There was at least one letter to Mac from an anonymous voter—a September 5, 1940 letter from an "Ardent Supporter." The four-paragraph letter said the author "knew Mac personally." He or she was "convinced the Judge was the best qualified candidate." "Ardent Supporter" focused on the candidacy of Henderson Stockton in the Democratic primary. The letter outlined, in some detail, several negative claims against Mr. Stockton, challenging his patriotism. The author noted that the recent lawsuit filed against Mac by Stockton was "far from impressive."

Mac wrote back to the address on the letter on September 8, 1940. He addressed the letter to "Ardent Supporter."

> We in our headquarters have known about the things in your letter, but have chosen not to even mention them. Even though my friend Mr. Stockton has

done the things he has done, and said the things he has repeatedly said, concerning myself. We don't campaign that way. I feel it is more important for Arizonans to know what a man stands for, than what he thinks about the other fellow. I am mindful of the fact that no man can gain high office in this state without lots of support from those he does not even know. If I don't know you, I hope to, and nevertheless now want to tender my respects to you, and my sincere thanks and appreciation.

That Mac refused to attack another candidate was one of the many things that catapulted him from a rural judgeship to national prominence. In today's political parlance, Mac always went high, especially when his opponent went low.

Publicity

For all of the twenty-first century, the term *media* encapsulates print, radio, television, Internet, blogs, cable news, and social sites like Facebook, Twitter, and Instagram. But in the 1930s, on the eve of World War II, media was simpler. Mac used print, radio, postcards, letters, posters, and gossip to accomplish two interrelated goals: to get his political positions out before the public and to turn his personality into publicity.

On August 23, 1940, in anticipation of a broad general campaign, John Murphy, Mac's campaign manager, sent out the first of many news releases. The line at the bottom of the one-page document said: "From: John A. Murphy, Attorney, Manager, McFarland for U.S. Senate, Title & Trust Building, Phoenix, Arizona."

While lost in history, the Title and Trust Building also took pride in having many of Arizona's best lawyers as tenants, including Irv Jennings and his partner Charles Strouss. Murphy's press release looked official:

NEWS RELEASE—DOUGLAS, ARIZONA, AUGUST 23.

A demand that, "we prepare to defend America now, not when it is too late" was made here today by Judge E. W. McFarland, Democratic candidate for

U.S. Senate. Judge McFarland, who is visiting Bisbee, Douglas, and Safford on a campaign tour, declared he favors "conscription of capital and labor as well as manpower" to put America on a preparedness basis. "We need action now," declared Judge McFarland. "When American leaders like William C. Bullitt say there is danger, Americans should not, like France and England, be lulled into a sense of security by listening to politicians who want to be elected to office and are willing to take a chance for our nation in order to further their special interests." Judge McFarland, a World War Veteran and long-time member of the American Legion, added, however, "God knows I hope the time will never come when we have to go to war, but if it should come, surely our youth will be better prepared by reason of the training resulting from conscription, than otherwise."

Mac thought highly of William C. Bullitt, Roosevelt's first ambassador to the Soviet Union. The United States had officially recognized the Soviet Union in 1933. In 1936, Roosevelt named Bullitt as ambassador to France, remaining until the fall of France to Nazi Germany in 1940. They had a good deal in common, and Bullitt had been very critical of those opposed to military preparedness as the looming war advanced in Europe.

In his news release, Mr. Murphy also told voters about Mac's position on two other important issues, the Copper Tariff, and the Colorado River. He put Mac "squarely behind the present copper tariff." And he quoted Mac: "The Colorado River problem has been a political football too long. Henry F. Ashurst, the present senator who is seeking re-election, has been asleep at the switch for 28 years in failing to obtain money for bringing Colorado River water to Arizona. What we need is action, not words."

The Remuda Ranch, near Wickenburg, Arizona, was one of the largest cattle ranches in the state in the 1920s and 1930s. Over time, the ranching world evolved, and many working cowboys found other ways to make a living. Today, the Remuda Ranch is a nationally prominent rehabilitation facility, specializing in treating patients with anorexia, bulimia, and other eating disorders. But in September 1940, Jack Burden was the owner and ranch manager. He oversaw a large cow–calf operation and was well known in Arizona business and politics. He wrote Mac a letter on September 6 and offered his perspective on Mac's campaign and his position, as stated in the August 23 news release.

Dear Judge McFarland, I have been following your speeches quite closely in the newspapers and have received your kind letter. I am certainly in favor of the various programmes [sic] that you have outlined, except for the confiscation of Capital, which isn't quite clear in my mind just what you mean. I don't mean to criticize, but only want to refresh our memories about painful experiences in the past; such as, the Government taking over railroads and making a miserable failure of it; the Government taking over the Air Mail and also making a miserable failure of that, and I think in the minds of each and every one of us is a grave question as to whether TVA is a Governmental success or not. It will take time to finish this story. I just write this because I was very much interested in your campaign. Very truly yours, Jack Burdin.

Two weeks later, Mac published a statewide ad in several newspapers clarifying his position on conscription. The ad was run by a large group of citizens, who posted their names in the paper. The ad quoted Mac on many things, including the sensitive issue of conscription.

Mothers and fathers call Judge McFarland neighbor and friend because he knows the defense of America depends upon a far-reaching program which includes training our boys to protect themselves and their country in times of emergency. Because he believes that conscription is the only fair and practical solution, and because he believes not only in the drafting of manpower, but industrial and financial resources as well. When sacrifices must be made, real Americans must be willing to make them without reserve, with special privilege for none and equal service for all.

Mac ended that ad, and many others, with words that made his case against Ashurst, without mentioning his name.

Judge McFarland is a true friend of all Arizonans. He possesses a thorough knowledge of the problems confronting Arizona. He will carry this knowledge to the United States Senate and give Arizona an active champion who wholeheartedly believes that his neighbors and friends should be represented by action, not by lilting phrases.

At two American Legion rallies in late September, Mac talked at length about his two decades in the American Legion and his unqualified support for increased resources and other preparedness issues. He forcefully challenged the Republican administration for its "twelve years of neglect to look forward to the future in protecting American citizenship." These rallies were conducted at Washington School in Phoenix and at the White Theater on East Van Buren Street. There was little opposition because Ashurst was still not very attentive to the challenge Mac presented. Mac also said, "It was not until the Democratic administration came into power in 1933 that an effort was made to build up our national defenses, a plea that has been made time and time again by the American Legion and other ex-serviceman groups."

Mac reminded his radio audiences that "ominous things are taking place across the Atlantic Ocean, but the Republican administrations of Harding, Coolidge, and Hoover failed to recognize them. And it was not until the invasion of Norway, Belgium, and Denmark that many of us realized the full import of such cowardly attacks. If you will recall, there were no Republicans prior to that time who stepped forward urging repairing our protective branches of government."

The written transcript of those two rallies does not reveal how good Mac was at using pauses, and letting audiences catch up, and think about what he was arguing. After one long pause, he said,

> Let's look at the future. During the 11-year period between 1922, the year of the Washington Arms Conference, and 1934, the year following the Democrat change of government, the Republican administration laid down only 35 combat ships. As a result of the disarmament conference during Harding's regime, there were destroyed or demilitarized 327 great ships, and during the last three years of the Hoover administration, not one single vessel was laid down by our government. Contrast that with the Democratic record of recent years up until June 1, when twelve new cruisers, two aircraft carriers, sixty-five new destroyers and thirty-six submarines, a total of 153 units being constructed in seven years. There is a naval picture. I hardly need to tell you about the army plans, for you and your families recall what took place last Wednesday when millions of America's manhood marched to voting precincts and registered

for possible training. Ever since this campaign got under way, I have been pledged to the building of an adequate national defense, and my stand remains the same. If elected to the senate, you can be sure that I will be an active supporter of every national defense movement. And you should return President Roosevelt to the White House.

Another unique way Mac delivered retail politics was "kicking the dirt" at farms and barnyards all over Arizona. His strongest farming and ranching base was in southern Arizona where, at the end of the 1930s, farming and ranching were big business. The driving issue was irrigation water.

Mac's campaign arranged a radio program in Tucson on August 28, 1940. Mac's campaign chairman, John Murphy, conducted a live, thirty-minute interview with three well-known Tucsonans. He introduced them to the radio audience. "Represented here are Mrs. H. C. Steffan, a housewife, Mr. John Goree, a farmer, and Mr. Kenyon Harris, a businessman. I'd like to discuss with you people some of the reasons Arizonans in every walk of life are giving Judge McFarland such a favorable reception." The radio question-and-answer session was carried in the early evening and covered more than a dozen topics.

Farmer John Goree said, "Well to begin with, Judge McFarland has been a farmer for more than twelve years. The members of his immediate family are farmers. He has firsthand knowledge of Arizona agriculture. He recognizes that if Arizona is to develop agriculturally, we must make full and efficient use of our water sources." Mr. Goree described, at some length Mac's service as the lead lawyer for the San Carlos Irrigation & Drainage District, and he spoke about Mac's years on the bench resolving the biggest water disputes in the state. "You know," he said, "Judge McFarland suffered along with the rest of us because we haven't enough electrical power for our needs. We can depend on him to work for the distribution of enough Colorado River power to supply our needs here in Arizona. And here's another thing. Mac says one of the biggest problems facing stockmen, like me, is security of tenure. If stockmen are to manage their ranches successfully, they cannot continually be subjected to changing regulations. The Judge stands in opposition to any measure designed to remove grazing from further areas in this state."

Mr. Goree likely could have consumed the whole half-hour radio show, but the businessman, Mr. Harris, also had things to say:

What Mr. Goree has just said also applies to both big business and small business here in Arizona. I know Judge McFarland and I know what he thinks—that both big and small business concerns are necessary to the American way of life. He feels that small businesses suffer more than large ones because of too much hasty and ill-conceived legislation in Washington. It is Mac's opinion that the obstacles placed in the way of small business can be removed. We want to make plans, build up our inventories, and expand without fear of regulations which are hardships for us. And besides, Mac believes the gains of labor cannot be maintained without setting up safeguards for business because the prosperity of each group depends on the other. Business and labor—they are together.

The "housewife," Mrs. Steffan, also had things to say:

Mr. Chairman, I think we should talk about national defense in addition to farming and business. This subject is vital to the future of America and close to the heart of all mothers. Judge McFarland stands squarely behind the American Legion's program and believes that a strong nation stands a much better chance of remaining out of war than an unprepared one! I know that because I know Mac is himself an ex-service man. He is only too familiar with the suffering, the death, the widowed mothers, and the orphaned children resulting from our participation in the last war. We were unprepared then, as now. We rushed into the conflict blindly and many of the tragic results, Judge McFarland feels, could have been avoided had we been prepared. I've listened to him. It is his considered judgment that our national defense depends upon a farseeing program involving the drafting not only of manpower, but of industrial and financial resources as well. When real sacrifices must be made, real Americans must be willing to make them equally and without reserve.

From the transcript of the radio program, it's clear that all three guests in the studio wanted to talk about another large part of Mac's campaign.

Harris said, "Mr. Chairman, there is another aspect that Judge McFarland has very strong opinions about. It is his observation that the effectiveness of the fifth column elements in undermining the resistance of other countries to invasion. He realizes that such subversive activities are only too numerous in our own country."

Steffan responded. "Mr. Chairman, Mr. Harris has expressed a thought foremost in the minds of mothers throughout this nation. We see war clouds on the horizon and many of our senators in Washington are doing so little to make our country secure. We are glad for Judge McFarland's stand on this matter. Our national morale must be high. Our patriotism unquestioned. Our motives sincere. When we permit foreign elements in our midst to influence our children's minds, to subvert whole groups of citizens, and to destroy their faith in democracy, how can we say we are safeguarding our national security?"

The chairman echoed Steffan's position. "Well, I know Judge McFarland well enough to be able to clarify this point for Mrs. Steffan. Mac realizes full well the logic of her position. He favors the deportation of fifth columnists and non-citizens who want to destroy our form of government."

Goree then made it personal. "We can be sure, Mr. Chairman, that in McFarland we will have a senator who knows our problems intimately. He never loses touch with people. I've seen cattlemen, sheepmen, businessmen, farmers, and merchants sit down in the Judge's chambers and talk over their problems with him. He is a patient and understanding listener. Because of that personal characteristic, he is thoroughly acquainted with the needs of the people of Arizona. When I say he's a patient listener, here's what I mean. He just has that human touch. He's sincerely interested in the other man's problems. I guess he's just made that way. He's easy to talk to, and always ready and willing to help."

18

Mac's General Election Campaign for the U.S. Senate, 1940

Mac's Republican opponent in the general election contest in 1940 was Irving A. Jennings, one of Arizona's most prominent lawyers. Jennings secured 5,487 votes in the Republican primary to soundly defeat his opponent, Burt H. Clingan. Mac won 63,353 votes in the Democratic primary. The Democratic primary total number of votes—111,612—dominated the meager Republican vote count, which stood at 6,509. Arizona was a solid Democratic state in 1940, and the state ticket would run alongside Franklin Delano Roosevelt's unprecedented fourth run for the U.S. presidency.

Still, Mac ran hard and took nothing for granted, not even an Arizona Democratic favorable vote count of almost twenty to one.

No Republican had ever won a statewide race for national office in Arizona. The Republican Party was perfunctory, known only for criticizing the New Deal, organized labor, and the egregious fact that Roosevelt's son was given an army commission. The Arizona results in that Senate race were never in doubt, but Mac used the nominal campaign against Jennings to bolster his expected service in Washington for the next six years. Just as Roosevelt carried America comfortably and won handily over Wendell Willkie, Mac won all fourteen counties and every major urban area in Arizona by a vote count of 101,495 to 39,657, a 60 percent margin.

The 1940 Senate election in Arizona came on the eve of massive changes in the country because World War II was raging in Europe. It marked the commencement of a shift from an older to a more modern era in Arizona's history and development. Capable men all over America were running for office to transition the country in the fall of 1940. Mac stood at the forefront of both environments—interpreting events and initiating legislation. His twenty-year effort to move up the political ladder in Arizona was about to serve him well. He used the general election campaign to establish his bona fides based on his record. He had endured the hardships of agrarian upbringing but had persisted under trying circumstances to become a teacher. He had endured the physical discomforts of a serious illness while in the navy, yet he emerged undaunted to create a new life in Arizona. He made providential decisions to continue his education, earning two degrees at Oklahoma and two at Stanford. While serving as a prosecutor in central Arizona, he endured great personal tragedy, losing his wife and three children to premature deaths.

He was a man of great internal strength. Even while serving as the Pinal County attorney, and superior court judge, working in private law practice, helping neighbors, and rebuilding his local church, he remained a farmer, never losing touch with the land, the people who cultivated it, or the crucial role of water in their future. At forty-six years old, he was in the prime of life with a clear vision of America's potential. He would become famous, although that could not have been predicted in 1940.

Irving A. Jennings, forty-two in 1940, was married to an elegant woman named Emogene. They had five teenage children. He was an outstanding lawyer and would, two years after the election, found one of Arizona's most prominent law firms, Jennings, Strouss, Salmon & Trask. Jennings ran an intense local campaign, stressing Republican positions but never challenging Mac's vision or his electability.

Mac was a candidate machine, devoting a good part of every day from early September to election day in November, pressing his and the Democratic Party's state and national platforms. He gave hundreds of speeches, radio interviews, and wrote and published scores of campaign mailers. He wore out campaign aides, not to mention at least two pairs of shoes. He wrote to hundreds of people and traveled to every county in the state, all the while sitting as a county judge. Every other judge in Arizona actively supported his campaign.

Mac's appearance changed over the course of the decade from 1930 to 1939. The leanness of his college and navy days had been maintained through the 1920s, but as he neared forty and after, he grew into a stocky, slow-moving man. At six feet two inches tall, weighing in at more than two hundred pounds and with a deep resonant voice, he was the picture of physical strength and health. He had a heavy shock of hair, just showing gray, topping a sunburned face.

"Got it campaigning," Mac said of his red complexion.

Maston Jacks, reporter for the *Tucson Daily Citizen,* said, "Judge McFarland's heavy shoulders and arms move when he starts talking. He waves his hand in an all-embracing gesture when he talks to audiences." Jacks reported on a story Mac told on the campaign trail.

"A voter said, 'Judge, I'm for you 100 percent. I'll vote for you and I've got an idea that may help your chances. Why don't you use somebody else's pictures on your campaign cards?"

Jacks said Mac was a good-looking man who had no worry over his campaign pictures.

The *Messenger,* a Phoenix newspaper, described Mac in a May 25, 1940, article:

> You'll be attracted to this man by his obvious sincerity and unadulterated friendliness . . . There is no sham or pretense about him . . . no theatrical gestures . . . a man of the soil . . . no grandstanding . . . a cow country judge . . . a dirt farmer who works on his ranch when he isn't presiding over the Pinal County Superior Court, or other courts . . . he has no illusions of personal grandeur . . . he is decidedly 'of the people' . . . he knows their hopes and ambitions . . . and their sorrows and tribulations . . . he's in the prime of his life at 45.

His grasp of language and a deep understanding of how politics actually worked at ground level were finely honed skills by the fall of 1940. His political biographer, McMillan, put it this way:

He displayed a "down home" country demeanor that many who first met him felt a bit unusual for a man of his position. He had a quick and interested mind, and carefully observed everyone's personality and concerns to every issue at hand. 'Dumb like a fox' served as a fair and frequent description of Mac.[1]

And for many reasons, not all of which are known now, he was frequently seen around Florence campaigning with Wimpy, his secretary's collie dog. He followed Mac all over town, in and out of the courthouse, church, movies, bars, and many other places. Mac loved that dog. With a grin on his face and an adoring look from the dog, he often said, "Can't get rid of him—going to shoot him someday," he joked.

His October 1940 general election speech was both a call to arms at the national level and a comprehensive statement about Arizona and its needs.

> I wish to take this opportunity to thank the people of this state for the vote of confidence they gave me in the primary election. I shall make it my job to see this trust is not misplaced. It is proper that we pull back the curtain of time, and review the conditions under which the Democrats took over the reins of our government seven and one-half years ago. We find a nation facing a great emergency. Our country was in the greatest depression since its inception. Idle factories could be seen everywhere. Farm produce was rotting on the farms and in the market places, while people were suffering because they did not have money with which to purchase them. Banks were closing their doors and people were losing their life savings. Mortgages were being foreclosed on homes and farms and people were being deprived of the homes in which they had reared their children. Nothing was being done to assist them. So great was the tragedy of the farmers who were losing their homes and means of livelihood that some of them used force to prevent Sheriff sales. Practically all mines were closed. The only one in Arizona that that was able to operate during that time was in my own county. Banks were struggling to head off the menace of financial panic.[2]

In mid-October 1929, middle-class Americans could see only prosperity ahead. Just a year earlier, President Hoover had announced soberly, "The conquest of poverty will be banished from this nation." While admitting not "yet reaching" that goal, he thought it was "within sight."[3]

Mac knew the context of such a bold statement. He came of age just as World War I was winding down. Mass production was assuming its place of dominance in America's industries. In 1929, Henry Ford sponsored the "Golden Jubilee of Light," honoring Edison and the fiftieth anniversary of the incandescent lamp. People were keeping up with the Joneses. Having two cars in middle-class garages was possible, so America thought. Walter P. Chrysler was *Time* magazine's man of the year. The world's tallest skyscraper, a sixty-eight-story colossus, was under construction in New York City. Thousands of Americans were turning to more speculative issues after making a little money on bonds issued as "Liberty Loans of 1918."

Little is known today how Mac and his family dealt with the stock market's crash on October 29, 1929. But it is safe to assume that they understood its gravity, while likely not appreciating what it would do to rural Arizona. When the New York Stock Exchange opened that morning, nervous traders sensed something ominous in the trading patterns. By 11:00 a.m., the market had plunged. Shortly after noon, a group of powerful bankers met secretly at J.P. Morgan & Co. next door to the exchange and pledged to spend $240 million of their own funds to stabilize the market. This strategy worked for a few days, but the panic broke out again the following Tuesday, when the market crashed again, and nothing could be done to stop it.

Before three months had passed, the stock market lost 40 percent of its value; twenty-six billion dollars' worth of wealth disappeared. Great American corporations suffered huge financial losses. AT&T lost one-third of its value, General Electric lost half of its value, and RCA's stock fell by three-fourths within a matter of months. It would take twenty-five years for the stock market to return to its precrash level following the 1929 plummet. Meanwhile, cruel but telling rags-to-riches jokes flew across the country: *Did you hear about the fellow from Wall Street who tried to rent a room? The clerk asked him whether he wanted it for sleeping or jumping. No, but I heard there were two men who jumped hand-in-hand because they held a joint account.*

Mac, like the voters he addressed in September 1940, had lived through the Great Depression that Herbert Hoover, Henry Ford, and Walter Chrysler could not see just eleven years earlier. And he could see dangerous times ahead:

> Nothing was done about these conditions by the Republicans, except that Mr. Hoover told us prosperity was just around the corner. Yet the national debt mounted four billion dollars during the Hoover administration, with nothing to show for it. Thus the Democrats took over the reins of government in distressing times, when our nation was facing this great emergency and the people were demanding that something be done.

Mac went on at some length in that first long address to all of Arizona. He talked about Democrats establishing the National Banking Law, "which insures deposits up to $5,000.00." Legislation for the farmer. Stockmen get a fair price. They should now get a more permanent tenure for their range, unhampered by too many regulations. The Homeowner's Loan Act saves homes. FHA loans enable thousands of people to own and live in "nice, modern homes." Now, he said, "the right of labor to bargain collectively has been recognized by the Democratic administration and is recognized in the 1940 platform of the Democratic party in this state and nation."

Mac mentioned but gave scant time to labor in that first speech. Labor was a big deal in the Midwest but of lesser importance in the Southwest. By 1935, workers all over America were persuaded of the importance of solidarity. Unionization had brought substantial gains to garment workers, coal miners, and newspapermen. John L. Lewis's United Mine Workers was a big organization, and they had helped Roosevelt win in 1934 and sustain the New Deal. But Detroit, the home of the biggest industry in the country, was virtually untouched by the rising tide of unionism. The American Federation of Labor, organized around craft unions, had no place for the skilled or semiskilled workers in mass-production industries. Until the beginning of 1937, there was little that resembled progress in the management-labor relations of America's four-billion-dollar motorcar industry. That industry employed 433,000 men and 18,000 women making cars, trucks, hearses, tractors, and ambulances. They all faced working conditions more medieval than modern.

Mac returned to safer ground after glossing over the labor issue.

Among other things which benefit Arizona, I pledge to continue the broad program launched for the coordination of river basins through reclamation and irrigation. In this connection, I wish to state that I made a trip to Washington, in the company of Senator Hayden. We visited the President of the United States and we told him of the desperate condition of the farmers of Arizona due to water shortage. There is insufficient water in our reservoirs. But for the pumping of water that practically all the farms of central Arizona do, Arizona would be a desert. Engineers tell us the underground water supply is being fast depleted. We told the President we must find a new water supply. The only place we can secure water from is the water in the Colorado now going down into Mexico. The President expressed a deep interest in the plight of all farmers in Arizona and has a full appreciation of their need for more water. He approved the efforts of the Reclamation Service to find a practical way to supply our deficiency with water from the Colorado river.

It is unlikely that Roosevelt knew how much Mac knew about water or the role that water law had played in Mac's life as farmer, lawyer, judge, and politician. He was very knowledgeable about irrigation, especially its history in central Arizona. In his part of Arizona, the Hohokam tribe inhabited the river valleys as early as 300 BCE. They developed irrigation via a network of canals diverting water from the Lower Gila, the Salt, and the Verde rivers. He was an expert on the formation of the Salt River Project, a product of the Reclamation Act of 1902. He litigated, as an assistant attorney general in 1922, cases involving water usage and irrigation issues. He consulted with legislators in 1922 regarding the Colorado River Compact.

Among scores of other water-law cases, Mac was the trial judge in the reopening of one of Arizona's most important water-law cases, Adams v. Salt River Valley Water Users.[4] In that and many other related cases, Mac examined Arizona's three sources of water—normal flow, stored, and pumped. In this most important case, Mac conducted the trial for several months and issued a twenty-six-page opinion in February 1937. His opinion was affirmed on appeal and stands today as bedrock law on water litigation.

Mac returned to federal law in that long general election speech.

> Another important step taken by FDR's administration is the Social Security Act. While it is not all we hoped for, it is a step in the right direction. Our old people never received any form of pension before the present administration. It is not adequate to give our old people all the comforts of life. I therefore favor an old age pension which will give our old people every comfort of life in their declining years and it should be paid for entirely by the federal Government.

The social security program Roosevelt's administration produced in late 1935 relied for its core principles on the concept of "social insurance." The Depression had many causalities. One of them was confidence in old institutions. Social changes that began with the Industrial Revolution had long ago passed the point of no return. The traditional sources of economic security, assets, labor, family, and charity, had all failed in one degree or another. Roosevelt choose the social insurance approach as the "cornerstone" of his attempts to deal with the problem of economic security.

Mac addressed other social and security issues in his general election speech. He argued for a higher standard of living for labor because

> [O]ur neighbors to the south have cheap labor. They produce copper several cents cheaper than we do in the United States. We have a tariff on copper to keep our mines from closing down. I favor a continuance of the copper tariff. I also favor legislation which will encourage the small mine owners of this state. I believe that many metals needed for war materials can be produced here in Arizona. The CCC camps have given wonderful benefits to the youth of our nation, taking them off the road, giving them employment, schooling and training, and enabling them to get jobs in private industries. Time will not permit me to discuss all of the constructive legislation enacted for the benefit of the masses.

His discussion of our neighbors to the south, Civilian Conservation Corps camps, and legislative goals are consistent with Democratic thinking and policies of the late 1930s. Roosevelt's administration had ushered in a decade of laws that Mac described as "liberal government and a better state of life for the masses of the American people." He used the phrase *masses* routinely during stump speeches and café discussions with constituents. Since the word generally implies "the common people," there is irony in Mac's use. While Mac was literally born in a log cabin, he was never common and never one "of the masses." He was extraordinarily well educated, well off, well spoken, and he survived his stay in a naval hospital for a year during the first world war.

With the Depression, national debt, farming, water issues, FHA loans, collective bargaining for labor, and the Social Security Act covered in the speech, Mac turned what he believed to be America's most important threat: "The outstanding problem confronting the nation today is that of adequate national defense. In Europe there are *ism* nations which recognize might and might only."

Mac's use of the term "*ism* nations" in 1940 reflected how both political parties viewed America between the great wars in Europe. He was talking about communism, Nazism, and fascism. An *ism* is used to form action nouns from verbs. It is useful in describing principles, doctrines, devotion, or adherence (i.e., barbarism, despotism). When Mac used the term, he was expressing a widely felt oppressive and discriminatory attitude.

He continued:

The *ism* nations have conquered small nations which believed in democratic principles of government, so dear to us in America, to satisfy their own greedy desires. We have seen Norway, Holland, Belgium and other small peaceful nations, who were trying to keep neutral, minding their own business, trampled by these powerful ism nations. Our forefathers brought forth upon this continent a nation conceived in liberty and dedicated to the proposition that all men are created equal. We have many liberties in our nation, cherished and loved by every American citizen. Our nation is again going thru a test as to whether it shall continue to endure. We must rid ourselves of the forces which would undermine our government. We have seen the result of their work in France, Holland, and Belgium. We have no place for the fifth column in the United States. Let us make the United States 100% American. And I may add, we have no place for the Communist Party on the ballot of this or any other state in the nation. I favor national legislation which will outlaw from the ballot the Communist Party or any other party which would overthrow our government by force.

Mac's fear of *isms* was a product of the times. His love of country and his fear of *fifth columnists* was felt by nearly all Americans. As Mac used the term, it meant persons who act traitorously and subversively out of a secret sympathy with an enemy of their country. Originally, the term described Franco sympathizers in Madrid during the Spanish Civil War. The origin was an allusion to a statement in 1936 that "the insurgents had four columns marching on Madrid and a fifth column of sympathizers in the city ready to rise and betray it." At the end of the 1930s in the United States, as involvement in the European war seemed ever more likely, Mac and many others feared the possibility of betrayal from within. They used the newly coined term *fifth column* as a shorthand for sedition and disloyalty. In June 1940, *Life* magazine ran a series of photos under the heading "Signs of Nazi Fifth Column Everywhere." In July 1940, *Time* magazine called fifth column talk a "national phenomenon."[5] In August 1940, the *New York Times* mentioned "the first spasm of fear engendered by the success of fifth columns in less fortunate countries."[6] One report identified participants in Nazi fifth columns as "partisans of authoritarian government everywhere," citing Poland, Czechoslovakia, Norway, and the Netherlands.

That Mac's central theme in the 1940 election was national security did not surprise his family, friends, or professional colleagues. He closed that first speech and many others before the November election with an impassioned plea.

> Let us not lull ourselves into a sense of security by saying that the warring nations of Europe will not come over here when they are now threatening us on the east and on the west. The only way to make ourselves safe from assault from the other side is to become adequately prepared. Then and only then will they recognize our might and our will to make our nation safe. We are now in the process of preparing ourselves. We have a president and leader, Franklin D. Roosevelt, who is able to see the grave dangers confronting this nation. He sees the only way this nation will continue is to have a strong

Army, a strong Navy, and a strong Air Force. The Democratic party stands for adequate national defense not for the purpose of sending men to the other side, but for the purpose of protecting us from assault from the outside. Not for the purpose of getting us into war, but for the purpose of keeping us out of war. Let us not be fooled by the Republicans and their leader, Mr. Willkie, who said in one breath of his speech in Phoenix that he was for adequate national defense and in the next breath that there were other things more important. I say to you there is nothing more important that the protection of this nation and the homes of our people.

Mac's Republican opponent, Irv Jennings was, speaking charitably, ambivalent about the likelihood of war involving the United States. He ran an ad on November 2, 1940, in every major newspaper in the state.

Place Patriotism Above Partisanship—EACH person appears below is a registered Democrat. They believe the problems confronting this nation today are of such importance that the interests of this state and this nation must be placed above party affiliations. They believe the best interests of Arizona will be served by electing Irving A. Jennings, Republican.

The ad read: "Are you are a Patriot or a Partisan? Now is the time to decide. Before America is recklessly plunged into war! The foreign policy of this country must be wisely and temperately shaped to prevent our boys from paying the supreme sacrifice for ghastly mistakes. This is a time for cool heads and courageous hearts. It is a time to place patriotism above partisanship. It is a time for America to send its most capable man to the United States Senate regardless of party label."

The ad ran two pages and listed the names of 205 citizens, each of whom was a "registered Democrat." They, Jennings said, "believe the problems of confronting this nation today are of such importance that the interests of this state and this nation must be placed above party affiliations. They believe the best interests of Arizona will be served by electing Irving A. Jennings, Republican."

There is little evidence in the historical record that the Republican Party in Arizona ever thought Jennings would prevail over McFarland. The GOP national platform for 1940 contained positions regarding the war in Europe.

The zero hour is here. America must prepare at once to defend our shores, our homes, our lives and our most cherished ideals. To establish a first line of defense we must place in official positions men of faith who put America first and who are determined that her governmental and economic system be kept unimpaired. Our national defense must be so strong that no unfriendly power shall ever set foot on American soil. To assure this strength our national economy, the true basis of America's defense, must be free of unwarranted government interference. Only a strong and sufficiently prepared America can speak words of reassurance and hope to the liberty-loving peoples of the world. The Republican Party is firmly opposed to involving this Nation in foreign war. We are still suffering from the ill effects of the last World War: a war which cost us a twenty-four billion-dollar increase in our national debt, billions of uncollectible foreign debts, and the complete upset of our economic system, in addition to the loss of human life and irreparable damage to the health of thousands of our boys. We declare for the prompt, orderly and realistic building of our national defense to the point at which we shall be able not only to defend the United States, its possessions, and essential outposts from foreign attack, but also efficiently to uphold in war the Monroe Doctrine. To this task the Republican party pledges itself when entrusted with national authority. In the meantime, we shall support all necessary and proper defense measures proposed by the Administration in its belated effort to make up for lost time; but we deplore explosive utterances by the President directed at other governments which serve to imperil our peace; and we condemn all executive acts and proceedings which might lead to war without the authorization of the Congress of the United States.

It is unclear in retrospect what the GOP platform meant by saying, "The true basis of America's defense, must be free of unwarranted government interference." It seems a contradiction of terms to say you're for an adequate defense only if it's free of unwarranted government interference. There was not then, nor is there now, a military defense directed, or funded by the private sector. Only the government can make war. In any event, the entire Democratic ticket won handily in the fall 1940 elections.

19

Mac Goes to Washington, DC, December 1940

While there is almost nothing in the archival records, Mac's move to Washington, DC, was almost surely organized by Edna and greatly enjoyed by Jewell. And while they did not intend to make Washington their permanent home as Henry Ashurst had done, the move meant a new life in a place that was as culturally and historically different as either Edna or Jewell could imagine. Edna would not work, and Jewell would face a big-city school system that bore no resemblance to the one-story school in Florence that she knew so well. There would be no more walking to school and no more lifelong friends. Paved streets, tall buildings, and a formal style unknown to either of them would enchant as much as it would confuse.

Mac would have resigned his judgeship shortly after the election, but he said he "needed the salary to live on, and pay expenses for the move to Washington."

Somewhat surprisingly, Mac revealed a little about "his feelings" and how the family felt about the move.

> Our getting ready and departing for Washington was mixed with happiness and sadness. We loved Florence and our home there. Our daughter, Jewell, had her horse, and hated to leave him. We didn't like the idea of leaving our host of

friends, especially for such a long distance, and for such a long time. And all of my immediate relatives lived in Arizona. My mother thought it was a long way for me to go away from home.

After that small reference, he returned true to form in his 1979 biography; only a little about family but a lot about himself and his new life as a United States senator.

Getting ready to move was a big job, but after family parties and goodbyes, the three of us left by train to Detroit where we picked up a new Ford car to drive to Washington. We were fortunate to have some close personal friends in Washington, Clarence and Mary Shotwell, with whom we spent several days after arriving. The question was whether we were going to rent a house, or live in an apartment. Edna made up my mind that we should live in an apartment, so we went looking. Clarence and I found one on Sixteenth Street, Northwest, which suited Edna. We managed to get it for six months. I thought she would be ready to move into a house by that time! And I was right. By the time six months had passed, we had purchased a modest home at 4404 Windom Place, Northwest, in which we lived as long as we stayed in Washington.

20

Mac on the Cusp of the U.S. Senate, 1940

On December 15, 1940, Frank E. Ross, a brilliant young writer for the *Arizona Republic*, wrote a long, comprehensive story about "Judge Mac, the Pinal County judge who had bested the Republican candidate, Irving A. Jennings. Because Senator Carl Hayden was not up for election that year, reporters like Frank Ross wrote at length about the new political team in Arizona. Mr. Ross wrote more like a poet than a reporter. And he wrote for a newspaper, the *Arizona Republic*, that had strongly editorialized for Irv Jennings and against Mac."

Ross had obviously interviewed Mac at length. He began his news story by relating a conversation Mac had while on a cruise ship crossing the Atlantic in 1935. Mac and his wife, Clare, were aboard the USS *George Washington* from New York City to London. Mac made friends with a fellow passenger, a Frenchman returning to his home from a visit to America. Ross captured the tone and significance of that chance meeting and tied it to Mac's remarkable win in the 1940 U.S. Senate race.

> The rising wind whipped salt spray across the steamer's foredeck—deserted except for the two men at the rail—and made the tall, slim Frenchman shiver despite his heavy overcoat.

"Shall we not go in and continue our talk there," the Frenchman said as he turned his face from the Atlantic swell and its biting breath, and half-faced his bright-eyed companion.

"O.K., we'll go in," the ruddy-faced man said, straightening his broad shoulders with a shake, taking one last look at the deepening troughs, and the soapy foam cresting with the mounting waves. Feet firm on the heaving deck, he stood poised for just a moment. "There is a lot in what you say about our government and its courts, and I'd like to hear more."

In the warmth of the vessel's lounge, some of the chill left the Frenchman's body, and the facile questioning of his interested listener launched a detailed discussion of land and the law, farmer and businessman, taxes and profits, depression and prosperity, waste and economy—all of the myriad factors which bring soundness or collapse to a government or a nation.

Ross captured what many, even some who were close to Mac, had missed in his remarkable political victory. It was a victory many Arizonans initially thought impossible. Everyone, except those who knew Mac well, and who sensed in him that rarest of all human qualities, the ability to question, listen, and build on lessons learned. Ross's newspaper story was already well known to lawyers, judges, and a few citizens in Pinal County. But his election made his personal story news to the whole of Arizona. In a few short years, Mac would become majority leader of the U.S. Senate, write the GI Bill, and have scores of pictures taken with Roosevelt, Churchill, Stalin, and everyone important in America. Ross's story was about a questioner, a listener, and a broad-shouldered Arizonan who drew out a shipboard companion, who would become a lifelong friend of his, albeit from afar.

During the long sea journey, Mac and his new friend explored common questions in the two countries related to land, the law, farmers, businessmen, taxes, profits, the Great Depression, prosperity, waste, and the economy. They exchanged views on the myriad factors which bring either soundness or collapse to a government or a nation. From the interview with Mac and Ross's other sources for the story, the fundamental nature of the man everyone called Mac emerged.

Ross's questions of Mac and everyone else he talked to covered both personal and political landscape.

What kind of a man is he? Does he really have the makins'? Does he expect to set the world on fire when he gets to Washington next week to take the oath of office as a United States Senator? What are his aims as a senator? What can he do for Arizona? Does he have a sane and wholesome slant on international affairs? Will he make a good senator?

All questions were answered and all answers advanced Mac's strengths and his chances for success at the national level.

Ross reported that "Mac would leave Pinal County for the District of Columbia with the necessary tools vital to success in national politics—he had perspective and a sense of balance. And he was clearly in the majority party." That year, Roosevelt comfortably carried the nation, beating the Republican nominee, Wendel Willkie, handily. Mac carried all fourteen Arizona counties and major urban areas, easily defeating the Republican candidate, Irving A. Jennings, by 101,495 to 39,657. Democrat Sidney Osborn won the governorship easily, and four-year incumbent Democrat John Murdock went back to the U.S. House. That overwhelming majority in a hard-fought general election meant he had the confidence of nearly everyone in the state. They believed in him without really *knowing* him. They knew what he said and what he said he stood for. But what "about the man, the inside of him," as Ross put it in his article.

Ross's extensive research into "the man" and the political discourse revealed seventy-six years later, discounted entirely his opponents' sense of him. He was most assuredly "not just a judge down in Florence, the town with the 'dobe buildings." That narrow view, Ross argued in his story, "would get you a totally false picture of the man, and the same holds true for a lot of the residents of Florence."

Decades later, Mac wrote his autobiography and reminisced about politics and running for office.

Anyone with ambitions for a political career should stop occasionally, look ahead, and determine what the next step should be. Should you quit, stay on in your present job, or should you aspire to another, perhaps higher office? The answer to this manifold question is usually personal to the individual and family; however, one is usually guided by lifetime ambitions. In this regard,

I do not claim to be different from the majority of those running for office. Ambitions frequently harken back to boyhood days. I well remember the time on the prairie farm when we labored long hours to get ahead. I had dreams of an education. I had always looked upon law and political life as honorable achievements.

To build his thesis about Mac, Ross examined the man of the moment by comparing him to the rest of Arizona.

He traveled more than most other Arizonans of the day. He'd been to all but three U.S. states. He'd visited eleven foreign countries—in this order: Panama, Cuba, England, Ireland, Scotland, France, Belgium, Holland, Germany, Canada and Mexico. Mark Twain, a man Mac had read widely, said in 1867, 'nothing so liberalizes a man and expands the kindly instincts that nature put in him as travel and contact with many kinds of people.' That perfectly defines Mac, at least by the time he journeyed from Arizona to Washington to start a new life as a U.S. Senator. Travel itself does not give perspective. But Judge McFarland made deliberate study of the peoples and their problems and their governments in the nations he visited. He transited the Panama Canal, knowing it would never have been built without Teddy Roosevelt's drive and persistence. He crossed the Atlantic in slow vessels. Ships with an air of comfort and informality, but not luxury, or upper class mentality. The people he met that way hastened friendships that would last a lifetime and continue to inform and expand his foreign policy views.

Mac, by everyone's take, was adept at making friends. For Mac, life without friends was like life without sun. He reveled in life in the sunbaked Southwest, just as he connected with, personally, almost everyone he met. He did it as easily as breathing in and out, and just as invisibly. That ship he took across the Atlantic, like the hundreds of trains, coaches, busses, wagons, and horses he rode was always a chance to make a new friend, and learn something he didn't know. He could make small talk, but he would move it from small to intimate discussions. He paused at inquiry and moved it to explorations about customs, feelings, realities and discord common to all people everywhere. And he searched for and logged in his prodigious brain, solutions to everyone's most common and frequently shared problems.

Ross asked Mac why he traveled abroad so often.

"Why are you so all fired interested in foreigner's views about the U.S.? Did you ask about the basic soundness of the American form of government?"

Mac said, "On the first long trip we took, I was amazed to discover that most foreigners know a lot more about the United States that we do ourselves."

"What did you make of that?" Ross probed.

"It started me making a closer study of America and sent me on visits to other states," Mac answered.

Everyone, from plain folks in town to law clients to litigants and jurors in courtroom cases, felt at ease with Mac. He had what Frank Ross called a "natural and likable simplicity." Without question, Albert Einstein was one of the smartest men in the world as it marched steadily toward World War II in 1940. But Einstein, like McFarland, was also a simple man. Einstein coined a phrase that would resonate for the rest of the twentieth century: "If you can't explain it to a six-year old, you don't understand it yourself." Mac understood simplicity and the need for simple, plain spoken explanations as well as anyone. But to simplicity, he added likability.

Frank Ross's story vividly captured the combination of personal traits that drove voters to Mac like honeybees to summer flowers. Ross poetically defined Mac on the cusp of the U.S. Senate just a few days after his story was published.

> Judge McFarland has rubbed shoulders with the world, he likes it, and is at home in any company.

Scores of Mac's inner circle in his 1940 campaign knew of Mac's childhood years on the Pottawatomie Strip in Oklahoma and how hard he worked on the family farm. They knew the core inner focus that drove Mac's political thinking. So did Frank Ross.

> A man who has picked cotton and chopped cotton himself, he can talk with a cotton picker and find interest and understanding in the things the cotton picker says. And with equal understanding and interest, he can talk to businessmen, university presidents, bankers and politicians. Mac's ability to talk to

everyone, those in the intellectual stratosphere, and those working the fields was legendary.

Dr. J. E. Wallace Sterling, president emeritus of Stanford University, put it this way:

> There is something about this man which ideals, a pioneer background, and self-supported education only partially explain. He has moral courage and an innate sense of good humor and judgment. He possesses a natural humility ('Call me Mac!'), which has to be experienced to be believed, yet is in harmony with the range and quality of his achievements. His demeanor, his conversation, and his personal correspondence are redolent with a rare homespun flavor which I, at least, have learned to greatly enjoy. As I have visited with him over the years, I have recalled again and again, the biblical line: "The salt has not lost its savor, nor the meat its strength."

Reflecting on Frank Ross's insightful writing about Mac, it is clear that he divined the essence of what explains Mac's move from his judgeship in Florence Arizona to his leadership of the United States Senate. Ross narrowed all the qualities of a world class politician down to two simple things.

> He must be steady and deliberate. Those basic elements of Mac's life gave voters a sense of Mac's balanced approach, and an early look at how he would perform in the U.S. Senate. The judge has it inherently. The chances of his being stampeded into anything are slight. He's the kind that looks before he leaps, steady, and deliberative.

21
Mac as Senator, 1941 to 1952

Mac took the oath of office as the junior senator from Arizona on the cold Friday morning of January 3, 1941. Four days later, inside the overly warm Senate chamber, Mac was ready to vote on eighty-nine weighty bills settling the destinies of two hemispheres. Mac was ready to vote, debate, and pass laws. He selected only Arizonans to serve on his staff. Out of his five permitted staff members, his first staff selection was a lawyer, Jim Walsh, who would later become a federal judge in Tucson. Then he asked Anthony Jones, a student at Georgetown Law to join him in DC. Two Arizona court reporters joined his staff, Wyly Parson and Charlie Powers. And last, but arguably most important, he asked his longtime judicial secretary, Mildred Larson, to round out his staff.

With a staff well versed in the law, Mac was surrounded by lawyers in the Senate chambers. Of the one hundred sitting senators, sixty-seven were lawyers, and forty-three came from jobs Mac knew well—veterans, teachers, and authors. There was one woman and one undertaker.

In his massive biography, McMillan devoted ninety pages to Mac's enormous record in the U.S. Senate. He comprehensively detailed Mac's federal legislative service in domestic and foreign policy. What bears repetition here are his colleague's comments about his Senate leadership.

Herbert O'Connor said, "Fellow Democrats were effusive in their praise. Mac's fairness and valuable ability to work out satisfactory agreements on controversial matters made him a standout."

Liberal Senator Hubert H. Lehman of New York, who had often criticized Mac, reported how well Mac could handle "serious difficulties ironed out due to the patience and great degree of skill with which the majority leader has handled affairs."

Emphasizing Mac's courtesy, consideration, and engaging personality, Tennessee's aging Kenneth McKellar said, "During the long time I have been in the Senate, I do not think we ever had a leader who has been more successful than the senator from Arizona."

Colorado's Edwin Johnson outlined Mac's role in representing his state. "A majority leader who never forgot that second responsibility. It has been closer to his heart than the honor he has achieved in the majority leader role more in the country's eye."

New Mexico's Dennis Chavez highlighted Mac's consideration of Native Americans. "Indeed, in him they have a friend."

Nevada's Pat McCarran related his concerns for mining interests, emphasizing Mac's "consistency and fairness."

Hubert Humphry praised the majority leader's work on "attaining civilian control of atomic energy, and great leadership in guiding us through the settlement of a most vital concern."

Washington's Senator Warren Magnuson selected social security as an area for praising Mac, "whose success in obtaining assistance in this field in the history of the Senate. They could not find a finer champion, or friend."

Perhaps the most significant were the words of Alabama's Lister Hill, who drew attention to Mac's successful efforts on behalf of veterans:

> In this field, the activities of the majority leader, the junior senator from Arizona, have been outstanding. He has sponsored and fought for the veterans not only of his own state, but for the nation. He has been farseeing and aggressive. Few in Congress, I believe, have a finer record of helping the men and women of the armed services, past and present, than Senator McFarland.

Alben Barkley, Roosevelt's vice president and president pro tempore of the Senate, talked about Mac in the larger context of his four-decade long service to the federal government.

> I know something about the obligations, burdens and responsibility of the majority leader. I wish to say that not since I have been in the Senate has there been a majority leader who has worked more diligently, more conscientiously and more successfully. It has been a pleasure for me as Vice-President to work with him and to give him any assistance within my power.

The July 1952 tributes to Mac were nearly as hearty from the Republican side of the Senate chamber. New Jersey's Alexander Smith thanked Mac for "the fine service which the majority leader has rendered to all of us, his uniform courtesy, and assistance." Senator Styles, the minority leader, held the second most important seat in the chamber: front row, center aisle, directly opposite Mac's. He rose in the chamber, saying, "I appreciate the excellent judgment of the Democrats in selecting Ernest McFarland as their leader because of his fairness, impartiality, courtesy, and kindness."

While Mac enjoyed nearly universal acclaim from every member of the Senate in 1952, none were more focused, or more thankful than Mac's whip, the young Lyndon Baines Johnson. What could not have been imagined in July 1952 was the historic match-up twelve years later, when Barry Goldwater challenged President Johnson and lost. Johnson's July 5, 1952, comments as Mac's whip in the Senate stand today as the longest and most complimentary statement concerning Mac's work in the Senate from 1940 to 1952. Johnson submitted for the *Congressional Record* more than sixty measures that Mac had introduced over the preceding twelve years. All sixty passed the senate. Forty were signed into law.

On July 5, 1952, Senator Johnson addressed a packed Senate chamber. His remarks about Mac are on record everywhere. They were, as was to be expected, expansive and salutary. However, Johnson's remarks also went to something that Mac had been known for his entire political life: trust. From Mac's first election in 1930 to his upcoming one in the fall of 1952, Mac would be the pinnacle of trust. While hard work, intellect, temperament, and a comprehensive worldview are all essential traits in successful politicians, trust is the hallmark of true political service.

In a famous letter Henry David Thoreau wrote to Ralph Waldo Emerson, he said, "When one confides greatly in you, he will feel the roots of an equal trust fastening themselves in you." Johnson's remarks about Mac indicate that Mac's selection of Johnson as assistant majority leader was based on the kind of trust Thoreau had in Emerson.

> Senator McFarland has occupied a difficult position and has acquitted himself well. He has brought to his post of leadership ability, talent, conscientiousness, honesty, and a spirit of co-operation which have made him liked on both sides of the aisle. His outstanding characteristic, however, is that he trusts the senate and the Senate trusts him. He is not one to block the will of the Senate. He is not a man who seeks to defeat legislation by indirect processes and by foreclosing opportunities to debate and vote. He believes in the democratic method, and he believes that the Senate is the sole judge of its own destiny. To my mind, this mutual trust between the Senate and Senator McFarland is the true success as majority leader.

Johnson told the Senate chamber a story that day that might be the only time in American history when both houses of Congress universally applauded what one senator had accomplished in just twelve years of service. He said he'd just spent a "quiet evening in my home the other evening with the Speaker of the House, Sam Rayburn." He reminded the assembled senators that Speaker Rayburn was rounding out his fourth decade in the house and had already served as speaker longer than any other man in history. Johnson said Sam Rayburn told him that evening that, "As he looked back over the years, there has never been before better co-operation, and greater trust between the two branches of Congress. That co-operation and trust exists because Ernest McFarland is one of the ablest, one of the most genuine, one of the finest men he has ever known."

None of the senators who served in the Eighty-Second United States Congress are alive today. It is not speculation to suggest than none of them, especially Mac, could have imagined the lack of trust, and cooperation within, or between the office of the presidency, the House, and the Senate in 2017. Mac would have shuddered to think that the legislative and executive branches of American government could ever have sunk to today's levels. It may have been the same shudder that Mac would feel in his upcoming battle with Barry Goldwater.

22

Mac and Barry Goldwater, 1952

Mac lost his seat in the U.S. Senate to Barry Goldwater on November 20, 1952. The big picture of that loss, as well as the painful details, are covered in McMillan's biography of Mac, written twenty years after Mac's death. In between the loss to Goldwater, and McMillan's comprehensive coverage of that tragedy, Mac published his own autobiography in 1979. By comparing Mac's firsthand account with his biographer's outlook on the matter in 2004, readers are given a glimpse of how painful and how unexpected that loss really was.

In his autobiography, Mac only mentioned Goldwater's name twice. Neither reference was penned by Mac. Both are embedded in an article written by Dick Waters, originally published in the *Kingman Daily Miner*, and incorporated by Mac into his book. Mac's own story does not contain a single word about the 1952 calamity. This is hard to understand at the abstract level. But his memoir is just that—a set of memories of good times, written twenty-two years after the second greatest loss in his life. Mac's decision to leave the loss to Goldwater out of his book is entirely consistent with his decision to avoid any substantive discussion of the loss of his wife and three children, even forty-nine years after the fact. Of course, the loss of family was very private, whereas the loss of his senate seat was very public. Nonetheless, both events are driven by the same powerful trait—take your losses privately and move on. When he lost Clare and the children, he waited it out and eventually found Edna and Jewell. When he lost his senate seat, he waited that out and eventually won the Arizona governor's office. Then he won a seat on the highest bench in Arizona—the Arizona Supreme Court. Classic Mac.

His 342-page memoir begins on the first page with "My life started on the rolling prairie of Oklahoma . . ." His final chapter, aptly named "Miscellaneous," includes a short piece written by a Phoenix lawyer named Powell Gillenwater. Gillenwater attached Dick Waters's two-page article. Nothing that Mac dictated to a secretary in 1979 mentions Barry Goldwater's name or the two times he bested Mac in a statewide election. Mac's autobiography ends with the Waters article headlined, "Triple-Crown Political Winner McFarland Is Proven Survivor."

Given Mac's intellect, certitude, and razor focus on his accomplishments in life, the "proven survivor" part of the headline may be why Mac ended his book with the Waters article. If nothing else, Mac was the quintessential survivor.

Readers are respectively directed to the McMillan 2004 extensive treatment of the political battles between Goldwater and Mac in 1952 and 1958. Goldwater ran an aggressive campaign against Mac, accumulating more than fifty thousand air miles in his travels about the state, during which he delivered more than six hundred speeches. He defeated McFarland in the general election by a slim margin of 6,725 votes out of approximately 260,000 cast, which Goldwater attributed in part to the unpopularity of President Harry S. Truman and the backing of popular Wisconsin senator Joseph McCarthy. Goldwater also launched a get-out-the-vote effort in the northern part of the state, knowing the margin of victory would be slim. He received very large financial support from Republican Party campaign organizations and several prominent party members.

When the Waters article was written on September 30, 1979, Mac was eighty-five years old, and the bitter defeat by Barry Goldwater had been softened by twenty-seven years of success in the governor's office, in the Arizona Supreme Court, and by a good deal of financial gain in the television business. Mac may have liked part of the tone Dick Waters used to describe the Goldwater win.

Barry Goldwater, Phoenix city councilman, rode the Eisenhower landslide to victory in the Senate race in Arizona in 1952, defeating McFarland by 6,700 votes out of 275,000 cast in an acrimonious campaign which featured the Korean War, President Truman and Secretary of State Dean Acheson as the major issues. It was that 1952 election that the Republican Party emerged as a powerful force in Arizona politics. Elected by the GOP were Senator Goldwater, Congressman John Rhodes, and re-elected was Republican Governor Howard Pyle and Republican Ross Jones as Attorney General. The election left the Democratic party in shambles. But out of the ashes of defeat, McFarland was not long in plotting a comeback. Some thought he started the next day, and he may have. But however he did it, two years later the Arizona-Okie came rolling back to ruin Howard Pyle's bid for a third term as Governor . . . Mac's survivor instincts emerged to assert themselves, and a few years later he was back in the thick of things, this time as an Associate Justice of the Arizona Supreme Court.

Apparently, Dick Waters interviewed Mac often over the years. In retrospect, especially given the Eisenhower coattails that Mac believed elevated Goldwater to his Senate seat, Waters secured a scoop without knowing it. During one of those interviews, Mac recalled a visit he made with General Eisenhower to visit the troops in Europe. This was shortly after the biggest engagement of World War II, the Battle of the Bulge, on the western front.

One time during the war when I was flying with General Eisenhower from Rheims, France, to some forward base, I told him that he was the most popular man in America. When, Mac said he asked Eisenhower, are you going to run for president? Then, Mac smiled and said: Ike looked at me and said "first I'll have to figure out whether I'm a Republican or a Democrat, won't I?"

While it's outside the scope of this book, the underpinnings of Mac's 1952 and 1958 losses to Goldwater seem clear today. Perhaps that's because hindsight is almost always right. McMillan wrote that those losses were "Mac's singular political defeat." That view is consistent with other national and historic coverage of the stunning return of the Republican Party to national prominence.

The GOP felt optimistic in 1952 because President Truman's popularity languished over the Korean War and the firing of General Douglas McArthur, domestic scandals, and economic problems. Republican expectations extended to gaining control of Congress, particularly the Senate. The GOP then held forty-six seats to the Democratic majority of fifty. If the GOP could gain three of the contested thirty-five that year, they would capture the majority. Their strategists targeted Mac for defeat, and they won.

Multiple sources credit Goldwater's win to a man named Eugene Pulliam, publisher of both Phoenix daily newspapers, the *Arizona Republic* and the *Phoenix Gazette*. As McMillan put it, "Pulliam waded into the upcoming political fracas with his shirt sleeves rolled up." The press extolled the advantages of a two-party state and urged Arizona to change its Democrat stance with a conservative mantra.

> MacArthur has made the greatest contribution of any man in our time to Christian civilization, and there is no greater advocate of freedom nor more violent opponent of communism than Eisenhower.

With Pulliam's backing, Goldwater fanned the flames. He accused Mac of failing to represent the state, warning of "creeping galloping socialism." Especially dangerous was the defection of influential Democrats Lewis Douglas and Stephan Shadegg, who switched sides for the 1952 race. Goldwater connected Mac to Truman and criticized "the deficit spending of the Truman socialistic left-wing control."

The September primaries in Arizona garnered Mac 108,992 votes in the Democratic primary—no surprise since Mac ran unopposed. Goldwater received 33,640 votes from the Republicans. That made it clear that for Goldwater to win, he had to win the votes of conservative and fence-sitting "Pinto Democrats." He had to lure more voters to the general election polls. The *Tucson Daily Star*, then the third-largest newspaper in the state, endorsed the Eisenhower-Pyle-Goldwater ticket, citing the Democrats at fault for allowing the nation to "enter three wars—Senator McFarland should be retired."

Goldwater outspent McFarland two-to-one, with 50 percent of his contributions coming from out of state. Goldwater continually kept the spotlight on Korea as the "war no one wanted to win." And he echoed MacArthur in advocating the use of Chiang Kai-shek's Chinese troops. The end result was a narrow defeat for Mac and the reality that, for the first time since 1920, Arizona would elect a Republican senator and governor. Mac was tied to the sinking image of Truman and the relatively unknown Adlai Stevenson. Goldwater won the support of the state's three major newspapers and had wide visibility in rural Arizona. Mac's down-home, country persona clashed with the more urbane and sophisticated style of Goldwater, Pyle, and a newly emerging conservative Southwest.

At the end of the campaign, two assessments of the result stand out. Ronald Bibolet, Mac's longtime loyal assistant, said, "The campaign was a heartbreaker. Mac was very much a methodical person and Goldwater was not. The Goldwater campaign was bombastic and he had the trends of time running with him through Eisenhower. But what defeated Mac was the absolute opposition of the two daily newspapers in Phoenix, who went after him with hammer and tongs."

The second assessment came from Goldwater himself. "I had no business beating Ernest McFarland, and I knew that from the day I started. But old Mac just thought he had it in the bag and just didn't come home enough. I could never have been elected if it hadn't been for Democrats . . . I'd still be selling pants."

Perhaps there is a larger Arizona lesson learned from the 1952 election. It ended the Democratic era while ushering in the Republican one. Arizona would never again be a Democratic state. While Mac was privately bitter about the loss, he kept quiet in public discourse. He felt partly at fault because he was overconfident and could not mount the aggressive, bombastic campaign it would have taken to beat a conservative Republican back then.

McMillan reported, "Those close to him noted a feeling of guilt that emerged in a fashion that could relate to his religious upbringing on the Oklahoma prairies. Mac gave up drinking alcoholic beverages, a pleasure he had long enjoyed."

Goldwater's surprise entry on the national stage marked the end of Mac's Senate career, but his colleagues on both sides of the aisle gave him a magnificent send-off. He was still the majority leader of the senate until January 1953. The Senate sent him on a goodwill tour around the world, which lasted six weeks. Edna joined him while Jewell stayed home in school. Along with honoring the outgoing majority leader and his wife, the trip had very functional aspects. Besides serving as a goodwill ambassador to the world, Mac also appraised postwar rehabilitation under the Marshall Plan. Underlying the entire trip lay a focus on the constant theme of maintaining a vigilant eye on global communist activity.

When he came back to Washington, DC, Mac performed his last formal duty in closing the Eighty-Second Congress and turning the reins of Senate party leadership to Lyndon Johnson. But Goldwater would continue to creep into Mac's thoughts over the years. Purposefully omitting his opponent's name, Mac obliquely referenced Senate years in his autobiography:

> Before the expiration of my second term in the Senate on January 3, 1953, I became a close friend of Senator Lyndon Johnson and his family. On the night of the 1952 election, when Eisenhower carried so many 'on his coattails,' Lyndon wanted me to contact the Democratic Senators in his behalf for the Democratic leadership. It doesn't matter whether one wins by riding on a coattail, or otherwise. In one loses, one loses. It soon became evident that Lyndon would be the next Democratic Leader of the Senate. I do not claim credit for this, but I was glad to see him elected. The question then came up as to what I should do when I got out of the office in January.

Mac mentioned several possible jobs in the near term, including work back in Arizona on the Colorado River suit against California, and a "movement started for me to bring about a merger of the international communications companies." His long-held interest in international communication issues won out. In essence, Mac became a lobbyist. "We arrived at a figure for my employment which was approximately three times the salary which I had received as United States Senator." Mac had an office in Washington, DC, and retained the services of Ivy Hackley, who had been on his staff in the Senate. The rest of his staff returned to Arizona. The goal of the federal job was to merge the big international companies. When that failed, Mac turned his attention back to Arizona.

23

Mac, 1954 to 1964

Governor, Businessman, Lawyer, Farmer, Grandfather

Up to 1968, Arizona's governors served only two-year terms. Mac ran for a two-year term as governor in 1954 and defeated Howard Pyle 122,235 to 111,399. After his inauguration on January 3, 1955, he successfully advanced bills in the Arizona legislature on health, education, and welfare benefits. He called the legislature into special session in October and December 1955. The October session revised the *entire* Arizona law code. The December session eliminated Arizona sales taxes on products sold to the federal government and instituted a tax on products purchased from out of state. These sessions, among other statewide consequences, opened the way for the Sperry Rand Corporation and other high-end companies to enter Arizona as major players in the state's commercial growth.

Mac served two terms as Arizona governor, from January 3, 1955 to January 5, 1959. He founded the Arizona State Parks System, established the Colorado River Boundary Commission, and significantly expanded state aid to elementary and high schools. He sanctioned the Interstate Oil Compact and pushed and signed new legal powers for the State Racing Commission. He also was a member of the National Commission on the Causes and Prevention of Violence from 1968 to 1969 and served as the director of the Federal Home Loan Bank of San Francisco.[1]

Mac inaugurated as governor of Arizona, ca. 1955.

The most unusual thing Mac did that first year was to appear before the U.S. Supreme Court as a lawyer. While the research is unclear, Mac may have been the only sitting governor of a state to argue a case before the United States Supreme Court. He argued Arizona's case, as co-counsel with John P. Frank, against California in its decades-long dispute over the Central Arizona Project.[2] The win in the Supreme Court kept the upper states from being enjoined, thus saving time for Arizona to push forward with the project.

In November 1956, Mac was reelected to his second gubernatorial term by beating Horace Griffin 171,848 to 116,744. These wins put Arizona back in the Democratic column. Mac decided not to run for a third term, electing instead to mount a second try at regaining his U.S. Senate seat then still held by Barry Goldwater. Once again, he lost to Goldwater, this time by a substantial margin—129,030 to Goldwater's 164,593. That win would carry Goldwater to his presidential race in 1964, which he lost to Lyndon Baines Johnson, Mac's oldest friend in the Senate.

The six-year period from 1958 to late 1964 were working years for Mac, but not in public service. He spent half his workweek in Phoenix running KTVK and the other half in Florence at his law firm and running his substantial farms. And, as McMillan reported, Mac paid more attention to his family, "particularly the growing group of grandchildren born to Del and Jewell Lewis."

Mac's company, KTVK-TV, Channel 3, was the ABC affiliate in Arizona for three decades. As president and chairman of the company, Mac exercised direct control over operations. The station met and surmounted many of the technology changes the television industry went through in the 1960s. It kept abreast of the financial needs for videotape capability, huge cumbersome machines that made the news and shows available, and the industry-wide switchover to color reproduction. Under his leadership, it also maneuvered its way through the legal and regulatory problems with the federal government. McMillan covered some of these challenges in Mac's political biography. "Mac mingled well with workers from electricians to studio hands. He propped up his feet on his desk while dashing off exuberant forceful calls to colleagues in Washington."

Mac's part-time law practice during the 1960s mostly dealt with agricultural and water-law issues. Upon his return to Arizona, he rejoined his longtime partner, Tom Fulbright, in Florence. In reality, Fulbright handled most of the firm's day-to-day cases. But driving down to Florence also gave Mac the time and enjoyment of farming and getting back to knowing everyone in town. He now owned four separate farms, although he had given his original farm to Del and Jewell at their wedding ceremony in 1952. Del oversaw all of Mac's farming operation in Pinal County, and he began "learning the ropes" at KTVK-TV as well. Mac was definitely a farmer rather than a rancher. He ran no cattle on his land and said, "Something always seems to happen to a man when climbs up on a horse. He thinks he's above everybody else and becomes a Republican."

His weekly visits to Florence also gave him more chances to see his ever enlarging "gang of grandkids." Kara was the first apple of his eye, born on April 11, 1954. Bill arrived on September 25, 1957, John on May 9, 1960. Then after a six-year rest, Jewell gave birth to Leah in July 18, 1966, and Dell Jr. on May 3, 1967. The Lewis grandchildren were the core of Mac's highly valued private life in the sixties and seventies. Both Del and Jewell became closely involved in the television station, balancing their time in Phoenix with the company and their time in Florence working the McFarland farms. Jewell, like her mother and Mac's first wife, Clare, taught at Florence High School. Edna mostly stayed at home in Phoenix and ran the large house without "in-house domestic servants," as she was known proudly to say.

Mac also shared with the grandchildren his love of travel. He and Edna frequently flew the grandchildren to eastern vacations. New York, Philadelphia, and Washington were often lecture opportunities for Mac. He made sure everybody in Jewell's family got to see some of things Jewell saw during her years "back east" while Mac was in the Senate. Cutting down on foreign travel during the sixties, Mac drilled "the American story" into his grandchildren. But he also made sure Edna, Del, and Jewell attended all presidential and state gubernatorial inaugurations with him.

He kept a close eye on state legal developments after his oral argument in the U.S. Supreme Court on the Central Arizona Project suit. This long case came to an end in 1963, when the U.S. Supreme Court finally ruled in Arizona's favor "eleven years after Mac, as majority leader in the Senate, initiated the law suit in Washington." Mac was justly proud of laying the foundation for that big win. Another five years would lapse before that bill would become law in 1968. By then, Mac would be Arizona's chief justice.

24

Mac and the Arizona Supreme Court, 1964

Mac moved up the ladder from lawyer to judge to supreme court justice in forty-four action-packed years. Save for legislative and gubernatorial stops, he followed an ever-steepening climb. During his climb, tens of thousands of lawyers joined the bar. Hundreds became trial judges. Scores became legislators. A handful became governors. But only fourteen men and one woman served on the Arizona Supreme Court between 1920 and 1964. Since only lawyers can serve on the court, Mac's competition in 1964 was probably less than a few thousand active lawyers. But the specific requirements for service narrows the list: Justices must be admitted to the practice of law in Arizona and be a resident of Arizona for the ten years immediately before taking office. Mac easily met those requirements, and his age and experience were complementary to his judicial election campaign.

Alexis de Tocqueville, in *Democracy in America*, famously said, "In America there are no nobles or literary men, and the people are apt to mistrust the wealthy; lawyers consequently form the highest political class and the most cultivated portion of society . . . If I were asked where I place the American aristocracy, I should reply without hesitation that . . . it occupies the judicial branch and the bar."

Mac was never an aristocrat, but he lived and sheltered among America's highest political class. Some might have speculated that, at age seventy in 1964, Mac had run his political gamut and ought to go home and sit on the porch for the rest of his life. They didn't know Mac. And if they did, they badly underestimated his voracious appetite for political office seeking. In 1964, Arizona still elected judges; that would change to an appointed system eight years later. And Arizona law would require judges to retire at age seventy. But for Mac, an open seat on the Arizona Supreme Court presented a last chance and therefore irresistible final run for office.

Jim McMillan's book sets the scene for Mac's 1964 decision to run for that open seat.

> Between 1958, when he lost the second senate race to Goldwater, and 1964 when Goldwater ran for President, Mac kept being mentioned as a potential candidate for this, or that position. His friends urged him to challenge Governor Paul Fannin. But Mac demurred and Republican Fannin kept a tight hold on the Arizona Governor's seat. The relative stability of the Arizona political scene fell apart in 1964 when Goldwater announced his candidacy for the Republican nomination for president. Governor Fannin, in turn announced he would run for Goldwater's senate seat. That same summer, Renz Jennings, resigned his seat on the Arizona Supreme Court to run against Fannin for the U.S. Senate. Mac's mind now called back to the 1930s and its memories of his constructive days in judicial robes. The hectic events of the ensuing three decades blew away the realities of the Great Depression and left pleasant reflections on the dignity of the law. Jennings's resignation focused Mac's political antennae on the Arizona Supreme Court.

The irony in these dominoes all falling at the same time must have been delicious to Mac. His opponent in the 1940 general election had been Irv Jennings. His opponent in the 1952 general election was Goldwater, who was now vacating the Senate, opening a Supreme Court seat because Renz Jennings—Irv Jennings's brother—would run against Paul Fannin. The same people, all running in different races, were about to collide in Arizona again. *Wonderful,* Mac likely thought. Both Jennings brothers would lose,

Goldwater would be out of the Senate, and Mac would sit on Arizona's highest court. Mac must have loved every minute of all of that.

This would be the first office Mac held where the formality of the judicial world would interfere with his chosen name. At the Supreme Court, his colleagues on the high bench called him Mac, but everyone else said either, "Your Honor," or "Justice McFarland."

Appellate courts often present as conundrums in America because they function so differently from lower trial courts. They are called *supreme* for a reason. Neither justice nor injustice ends with a jury verdict or a trial court's judgment. Civil and criminal litigants have rights to speedy trials, to challenge unfavorable verdicts, to change the common law, and to appeal their cases to higher courts. While most trial court results affect only the litigants in a particular case, appellate courts have much broader impact.

Ordinary citizens, not to mention some U.S. presidents, either misunderstand or fail to appreciate state and federal courts of appeal. They can change the law. They can change the outcome in a single case or an entire class of cases. But they cannot review the issues without due deference to the lower court judge and the actual record on appeal. The target for the appellant, the party bringing the appeal, is one or more errors by the trial judge or fundamental error by the jury. The solace for the appellee lies in knowing that some deference must be paid to the lower court.

Appellate courts are instinctive about fairness due both to the trial judge and the appellant. One overarching principle of appellate law is that the trial judge should have a clear first chance to address issues later brought up on appeal. Issues not properly preserved in the trial court record below will be ignored on appeal unless a gross miscarriage of justice would ensue. At nearly the 100 percent level, lay persons do not understand how appellate courts work, or why they have such unadorned power to change the law.

Mac had an advantage rarely seen in supreme court elections at the state level. He had forty-four years of experience in prosecuting, defending, judging, and making law. Few Supreme Court aspirants could match his record.

Governor Fannin had appointed a Tucson Republican, Edward W. Scruggs, as an interim justice to fill out Renz Jennings's remaining term. Scruggs campaigned by buying billboards and TV time. But campaign aides misinformed Mac about filing dates, so Mac was too late to buy time, even at his own TV station. So, Mac ran against the incumbent, Scruggs, the same way he'd conducted all of his other political races, "automobile and shoe leather campaigning in the small and large towns across the state." He made campaign appearances in every significant town except Page and Bagdad. As James McMillan put it, "he walked the streets, shaking hands, in and out of barbershops, groceries, laundromats, service stations, and bars, always extemporizing on park benches and under main-street shade trees."

He beat Scruggs by a vote of 199,494 to 135,468, the highest percentage for any opposed candidate in the 1964 Arizona election. To his great surprise, his total marked the largest number of votes he had ever received in *any* election in his career. When the election results were announced, Mac was asked how he wanted to be addressed—Senator, Governor, or Mr. Justice. Mac said, "I'd just as soon be called Mac. You fellas get stuffier and stuffier as I get older." The post-election TV commentary said it all:

> At seventy, Mac is showing results of a lifetime in the political arena. The brisk, sometimes hurried gait of other campaign years, which saw him barnstorming the state is now a deliberate stroll. The handshake is still warm and transmits a sincere feeling, but it is not the bone-crusher of the old days. But a few moments of conversation reveals, even to a stranger, that behind a pair of eyes whose sparkle belie their age, rests the same steel trap mind that, for almost half a century, has guided one of the State's most outstanding careers before the bar, at the polls, and on Capitol Hill.

The 1964 Arizona election was a trifecta for Mac. He was thrilled to watch President Lyndon Baines Johnson trounce his nemesis, Barry Goldwater, in the national election. Goldwater only won 52 electoral votes to Johnson's 486. This was the largest popular vote margin in American history. Johnson beat Goldwater 61 percent to 39 percent. Mac attributed the results to Goldwater's "trigger-happy image in foreign affairs and his identification with such groups as the John Birch Society."

He was almost as thrilled when the governor's office in Arizona returned to Democratic hands when Sam Goddard beat Lieutenant Richard Kleindienst.

When he assumed Arizona's highest bench on January 4, 1965, he took the oath of office in front of the old state capitol building, the same spot

Mac as chief justice of Arizona.

where, ten years earlier, he had been inaugurated as governor. He joined four old friends on the court—Chief Justice Jesse Udall, Justice Fred Struckmeyer Jr., Justice Lorna Lockwood, and Justice Charles Bernstein. Mac served six years on the Arizona Supreme Court and as chief justice from January 1, 1968, until December 31, 1968. He served as acting chief justice part of the prior year.

There are hundreds of stories about Mac's service as Arizona's chief justice. Arguably, he was the hardest-working chief justice the state ever had. But a story that speaks volumes to Mac's style, his loyalty to old friends, and his sense of humor, is one Dick Silverman remembers vividly. Dick, now a prominent lawyer and civic leader, was one of Mac's first law clerks. Fresh out of law school, Dick had no legal experience and little knowledge about Mac's long career as a country lawyer. But he noticed that Justice McFarland often had visits from old friends from Florence. They seemed to have wide-open visiting privileges and would saunter into his chambers through the open door that Mac always had. After one old friend left, Mac called Dick into his chambers and told him he would have do something unusual, because Mac was too busy that day to do it himself. Mac told Dick that he wanted him to fix a traffic ticket that his old friend had brought in that morning. Dick had that awful feeling that comes to every lawyer when faced with what seemed to be an obvious breach, if not an actual crime. Dick resisted, saying he could not do that.

"Why, not, Mr. Silverman? I've been fixing traffic tickets for some old cronies from Florence for years. You know how I do it?" Mac had asked.

"No, Your Honor," Dick said.

"I pay them, of course. Now I'll give you the money, and you go to that traffic court downtown and pay the fine."

Mac wrote scores of supreme court opinions. But his tenth supreme court opinion would become nationally famous. At the time he wrote it, in 1965, it was not controversial. It was a correct statement of the law. It was about an issue that very few people in America paid any attention to. It would, just a year later in June 1966, become highly controversial, change the law, and be remembered to this day as the instigator in expanding the Bill of Rights to every American. The case was *Miranda v. Arizona*.

Mac's opinion would be overruled by the U.S. Supreme Court, and American law enforcement would change for the better forever. James McMillan devoted nine full pages of Mac's political biography to the *Miranda* decision. *Miranda* was Mac's most significant reversal by the Supreme Court. But it was not his only case the high court overturned.

They also reversed him in the *Lassen v. Arizona Highway Department* case. In hindsight, it is possible to rationalize both reversals as differences in how Mac saw the law. He was as strict a constructionist as there could be. The majority on the U.S. Supreme Court was not. Mac viewed constitutional litigation through a very narrow lens—one where judges only applied the law; they had no role to play in making it. The court saw the law as an evolving assessment of constitutional law. In both cases, the U.S. Supreme Court overturned him because Mac's narrow construction did not allow for changes that met modern standards in due process of law.

Mac's Arizona opinion on Ernesto Miranda was carefully drawn, covered twenty-one pages of existing law, and summarily rejected Miranda's claim that his confession had been improperly admitted in evidence. Mac accepted without question the testimony of the arresting officer, who testified that he had "informed the defendant of his legal rights and that any statement he made might be used against him." Mac saw the only question in the jury verdict in the trial court as whether there was a violation of the Sixth Amendment by admitting the confession made outside the presence of an attorney. Mac's Arizona Supreme Court opinion was typical of his judicial philosophy and his writing style—a masterpiece of directness.

> We hold that a confession may be admissible when made without an attorney if it is voluntarily and does not violate the constitutional rights of the defendant.

The U.S. Supreme Court's sixty-three-page opinion defined the case as a violation of the Fifth Amendment because the defendant made the confession without knowing he had a right to remain silent or that he had the right to an attorney during his interrogation. In its 1966 decision, the U.S. Supreme Court expressly overturned the Arizona Supreme Court in equally direct language.

> The Supreme Court of Arizona held that Miranda's constitutional rights were not violated in obtaining the confession . . . In reaching its decision, the court emphasized heavily the fact that Miranda did not specifically request counsel. <u>We reverse</u>. From the testimony of the officers and the admission of the State, it is clear that Miranda was not in any way apprised of his right to consult with an attorney and to have one present during the interrogation, nor was his right not to be compelled to incriminate himself effectively protected in any other manner. Without these warnings, the statements were inadmissible. The mere fact that he signed a statement, which contained a typed-in clause stating that he had "full knowledge" of his "legal rights," does not approach the knowing and intelligent waiver required to relinquish constitutional rights.

Mac decided in the spring of 1970 he would end his half-century career in public service. He would retire at the end of his term. As justice and chief justice, he wrote more than 320 full opinions, some of which were nationally important. That raw number far surpassed any other contemporary justice.

His exit on January 4, 1971, was described by a well-known lawyer and court watcher. "You are indeed the greatest justice our court has ever known."

Bernie Wynn, an *Arizona Republic* reporter, asked for the secret of his success. Mac said, "I'm leaving office, not retiring. I always make it a point to enjoy my work no matter what." His wife, Edna, quipped, "It's because he could never hold a grudge, no matter what."

One of Arizona's best lawyers, Mark Wilmer, summed up Mac's judicial career in six words. "Humility, fairness, integrity, absolute confidence, and trust."

John Moran, his longtime friend and law clerk, regarded Mac as "in the August of his years with no more mountains to climb and no more political peaks to achieve . . . kind, gentlemanly, he loved the law."

Stanford Law Dean Charles Meyers wrote, "To say Ernest W. McFarland has left a lasting mark on the interpretation and application of the law in Arizona is indeed an understatement. His well-reasoned opinions, personal integrity, and years of exemplary public service have set standards for all judges, lawyers, and politicians to ascribe to."

His lifetime friend, Justice Fred Struckmeyer Jr., may have said it best.

> He brought with him an awesome knowledge of government from the township level to the level of the Executive of the U.S. and all stops in between . . . He could relate to the average citizen even in a complex legal case . . . Mac was versatile—going from legal purist to a sympathetic and understanding jurist— not easily matched. The judicial system of the State of Arizona is fortunate that Mac passed our way.

When he walked from the state capitol on his last day, Mac said, "You just have to keep going and that is what I hope to do."

25

Mac's Grandchildren

Many of Mac's titles were the consequence of hard-fought battles in electoral trenches. But Mac's title—grandfather—was his favorite. His five grandchildren and seven great-grandchildren became, each in their own way, his new voters—his constituents, the people he was bound to serve in his dotage. His grandfatherly duties came about, in part, because Jewell, his adopted daughter, was always the apple of his eye. She turned out to be brilliant and compassionate and became the chief-steward of the McFarland legacy. While her children all proudly bear the name Lewis, they are McFarlands if not by birthright, by how they grew up and how they feel about the grandfather they all called Mac.

Their grandfather was Arizona's favorite son, a fact only belatedly made known to them. As children, they didn't know his politics, his leadership, his stewardship of laws and rights, or his legacy. They just knew he loved them as much as they loved him. Jewell's children, Kara, Bill, John, Leah, and Del Jr., all advanced the family legacy in ways Mac never saw. One can only imagine how chest-thumping proud he would have been. They didn't see him in awe. They just knew he loved them and they loved him. He may have been Arizona's favorite son, but they all thought he belonged to them. They are all well educated because he insisted on that. They have good manners, are well traveled, show respect for everyone, and are exceedingly polite. They treat their friends the same way Mac treated them. And they are fierce advocates for his legacy.

John Lewis is the president of the McFarland family foundation.[1] His siblings gave him the honor and the job of leading the effort to advance Mac's legacy. Their combined efforts, under the auspices of the McFarland Restoration Fund, resulted in the rebuild of their grandfather's memorial at the Wesley Bolin Park at the Arizona State Capitol in 2015. They give substantial credit to Vince Murray, a noted Arizona historian, and Don Ryden, a well-known historical architect, for the resounding success of that project, which is literally and figuratively a walk through their grandfather's entire life.

The grandkids called their grandparents "Grammie and Mac." They all grew up in Florence on the farms Mac started. Whether there, or at the McFarland home in Phoenix, the visits between Mac and Jewell, and their adult grandchildren were mostly one-on-one and personal. *How's your schooling?* School was extremely important to Mac. *What's going on in your life?* These were the main topics that dominated their conversations. Sometimes Mac would share a story or experience here and there about his life and career. That sharing made the grandchildren feel special in a way they wouldn't really understand until after both "Grammie and Mac" had passed.

The Lewis clan, children of the fifties and sixties, knew little about Mac and Clare's life together in the 1920s. The McFarlands of the 1920s wore funny hair styles—bobbed for women, slicked back for men. The Lewis children missed the birth of jazz and blues, but were fired up by rock 'n' roll. The younger generation in the roaring twenties probably did not roar all that much in Florence, but they had bootleg liquor and cigarettes rather than marijuana and LSD. The youth in Florence didn't know much about territorial Arizona. They heard about flower children in San Francisco and college resisters in the seventies. But they didn't know the Jazz Age their famous grandfather lived through or irrigation farming south of the Gila River.

Generational differences don't change how grandkids feel about grandparents. The Lewis grandkids loved Mac and Grammie without knowing the role Mac, Edna, and Jewell played in Arizona history.

All the grandchildren treasure their memories of trips with Grammie and Mac. One of those trips happened in the summer of 1970. John was ten and a fifth grader in Florence. His older brother was twelve. That's the year Grammie and Mac took them on a summer trip to New York City. They flew to New York City, then took a train down to Philadelphia, then on to Washington, DC. The boys remember their grandparents as "quite the tour guides, as they tirelessly took us to see all the major sights in each city. We visited Independence Hall in Philadelphia. The uniformed tour guide was explaining the historical significance of a big room by saying, 'This is where Patrick Henry gave his famous speech and said, "Give me liberty or give me death."'" John asked Grammie, "Which did he get?" They chuckled, but were particularly happy that a ten-year-old was paying close attention to American history.

In Washington, DC, Mac took the boys to see all the major sights, "but as an added bonus we got to join Mac as he made calls on some of his old political friends who were still in office. We went to the House of Representatives and met Speaker John W. McCormack." John does not recall the conversation but was mesmerized by the huge crystal chandelier hanging from his office ceiling. Later, as they walked through the front lobby of the U.S. Capitol, John and Bill were walking behind Mac. He approached a door, and they all went into a large room. It was the floor of the U.S. Senate. A security guard stepped in between them, and asked "May I help you?" Edna told the boys, "We have to go upstairs where the families go." John was taken aback by the blunt belligerence of the security guard. "I wished, at the time," he later said, "I had said, 'Give me liberty, or give me death!'"

When Bill and John were in high school, Mac often drove down to Florence, picked them up, and took them to his farms. John remembers one of the more monumental trips. "Mac introduced us to his farm manager. He told him to measure off forty acres of one of his large fields, and plant cotton for myself and brother Bill. Mac said, 'This will be twenty acres for you and twenty acres for Bill, but it will not be separate. You and your brother will be fifty-fifty partners in this forty-acre cotton project.' The cotton was planted late in the season, and then someone forgot to apply preemergent herbicide so the weeds almost took over our crop. However, Mac paid all of the expenses, and Bill and I got the revenue. What a deal for us! Bill and I now had accounts with the River Cooperative Cotton Gin as well as the Cotton Marketing Cooperative for California and Arizona. Bill and I were now cotton farmers!"

Jewell McFarland Lewis, ca. 1950s.

Jewell could not have been more like Mac even if she had been his biological rather than his adopted child. In retrospect, Jewell McFarland Lewis may be the poster child for how environment and nurturing takes hold, entirely without genetic influences. Her obituary described her as an "incredible leader, mentor, and friend who dedicated her life to making Arizona a better place to live." Mac would have been thrilled to know that, but it was exactly how he thought she'd turn out.

Jewell joined the Kappa Kappa Gamma sorority at the University of Arizona in 1946, earned her bachelor's degree in 1950, and then returned to Washington, where she earned a master's degree at George Washington University in 1952. In 2002, she was profiled in *The Key* as a "Media Mogul and Philanthropist." Her "commitment to one was integral to the other," the magazine said. By then, Jewell was the chairman of the board of Media America

Communications, Inc. It is not by accident that the company's acronym was "MAC." It was the parent company of one of the largest ABC-network-affiliated television studios, two popular FM stations, the azfamily.com website, *Phoenix* magazine, and Desert Production Center, Inc.

Prior to Mac's death in 1984, KTVK, Channel 3, was the ABC affiliate in Arizona and had been since Mac began the station with three friends in 1954. It lost the affiliation in 1995, but Mac's local station continued to go head-to-head with the national network stations in Phoenix.

Jewell's most important personal endeavor was her founding of the Jewell McFarland Lewis Fresh Start Women's Resource Center in Phoenix. It was a self-help center, providing assistance and resources to women of all ages with counseling, mentors, training, and contact with local social service organizations.

Jewell's youngest daughter, Leah Lewis Hendriske, an Arizona State University graduate and a member of the Kappa Kappa Gamma sorority, said, "Our family has been blessed with a caring and giving lady. Not only has she given of herself to the community and the state, she has always been there for every member of the family."

Jewell frequently told people about the most exciting day in her life. When she was eleven, Mac pulled her out of school one day and hustled her to the nation's capitol building. She was in the gallery when Franklin Delano Roosevelt gave his famous "a date which will live in infamy" speech to her father and forty-eight other U.S. senators on the floor of the Senate chambers. While she vividly remembered that day, she also said that one of her most influential moments was when Mac made her promise to return to Washington and complete her master's degree before marrying her childhood sweetheart, Del Lewis. Her bachelor's degree from the University of Arizona begat the master's degree from George Washington University, which in turn begat her doctorate in education from Arizona State University. After teaching high school in Florence, she became the reading director for Coolidge public schools. That naturally led her to many national committees, all related to education. Remarkably, she held active memberships and contemporaneous memberships on the Governor's Advisory Committee on Quality Education, the Arizona Education Foundation, and several boards of all three state universities in Arizona. She was the only woman on the Power

Authority Board. She and her husband, Del, endowed two university chairs, one in Mac's name, and the other in the Lewis name, at all three Arizona universities.

Jewell is famous for maintaining a simple but strong message to everyone she came in contact with: "Every child in the United States ought to have the opportunity to get a good education."

That was the message she preached to her five children and her seven grandchildren, all of whom are college graduates.

While all five of the grandchildren were Mac's favorites, the middle boy, John, shared one particularly poignant memory. Toward the latter days of Mac's life, John frequently visited Mac at his Phoenix home. These visits were "mostly to get him out of the house." Often they would drive down to Florence so Mac could see his farm. On one trip, when John and Mac were driving back to Phoenix, Mac had been napping on and off in the car. John remembers Mac going in and out of periods of confusion.

"Nothing nutty, just foggy unclear awareness as Mac was dozing in and out of his little naps. We were headed home passing through the small town of Coolidge when Mac awoke, and asked where we were. 'Coolidge,' I said, where I went to high school. Mac asked if we could go by and visit an old friend named Ben Arnold. Ben Arnold was the justice of the peace in the area, a judge that had gotten me out of a speeding ticket or two. Back when I was in high school, I got a ticket on the outskirts of town, I took it in to Ben Arnold and showed Ben that the deputy sheriff wrote down that my pickup truck was a Ford, and not a GMC, which it was. Ben gave me a big smile and said, 'Don't worry, John, I will take care of this. Now, how is your grandfather doing?' Ben thought the world of Mac and many of the locals knew it. Ben told me that when Mac first moved to Florence, Ben was his roommate. Ben continued to tell me stories of the interesting people Mac represented in his early days."

John continued his story.

"We are in Coolidge?" Mac asked as he awoke from another short nap.

"Yes," John replied.

"Can we go by and visit Ben Arnold?"

John wasn't sure where Ben lived and tried to talk Mac out of it.

"I heard that Ben's wife died, and I would like to see him," Mac said.

"I'm not exactly sure where Ben lives," John said.

Mac replied in a sad, soft voice, "Well, John, it's up to you." John remembered, "Those words were like the golden magic words to my soul. I immediately turned the car around and told Mac that I wasn't sure where Ben lived but I had an idea and at worst we could find out. We pulled up to a house, I walked up, and knocked. Ben Arnold's daughter-in-law answered the door and I told her who I was and that Ernest McFarland was in my car and wanted to see Ben Arnold. She gave me a big smile, and pointed to a house kitty-corner across the street. She said, 'Ben lives there.' I got back into the car with Mac, I told Mac that Ben lives right over here across the street. As I was relocating Mac and his car over across the street, Ben's daughter-in-law quickly gave Ben a call and alerted Ben that he had a visitor coming.

"As we pulled up onto Ben's driveway, Ben came running out of his house shouting 'Mac! You don't have to get out of the car, I will come to you.'

"I rolled down Mac's window on the front passenger side of the car as Ben came to greet his lifelong friend.

"Mac said to Ben, 'Ben, I read in the paper that your wife had passed away and I want you to know that you have my deepest sympathy.' Ben thanked him, and they started reminiscing about old times. Ben was fired up about politics recalling the nasty tactics that Mac's political opponents had played on him over the years. Mac just stared off into a leafless dormant tree. It was January. This was a very touching scene for me to witness; two very old friends holding hands, tears in their eyes knowing that their time on earth was very near the end. After their good-byes, Mac and I started our hour-and-a-half-long journey back up to Mac's home in Phoenix. Mac seemed preoccupied as he seemed to be deep in thought, just staring ahead. I said, 'Wow, Mac, Ben sure doesn't seem to like the Phoenix newspaper guys saying that God is going to have to preheat their cells in hell when they die.' Mac just answered, 'Yeah, ole Ben. He has always been quite the character.'"

Mac's grandchildren have hundreds of stories about him. They remember him always teaching them something. They don't remember him lecturing or instructing them, but they remember how he taught by example. Perhaps the best of those stories is one John remembers vividly.

"As a youngster, Mac had a heavy hand in teaching me right from wrong. Sometimes he would teach by telling me, but the loudest method Mac had was his example. I knew that Mac would never ask me to do something that he himself would not do. For example, one time my family was up in Phoenix at the Good Samaritan Hospital. I was a seven-year-old and was playing around in the main lobby as my prematurely born baby brother was being incubated in the children's ward because of underdeveloped lungs. I went up and rattled the newspaper machine, and a whole bunch of quarters came tumbling out. I took my newfound treasure to inform my grandfather of the streak of luck I had. Mac said, 'Here, give me those.' Mac went over to the newspaper machine and put each quarter back in one by one. Nothing more was ever said, that was it. I got Mac's message loud and clear."

Kara Lewis, Mac's first grandchild, remembers him when she was "just a baby. He was eating sugar and butter at Grammie and Mac's home in Phoenix." Like his other grandkids, Kara got her educational trip back to New York City, Philadelphia, and Washington, DC. But rather than the U.S. Capitol or Independence Hall, Kara remembers him taking her to see *Fiddler on the Roof*. Her funniest memory of him is catching him "dressing up as

Mac and Edna with their first two grandchildren, Kara and Bill, ca. 1957.

Santa Claus in his bedroom on Christmas Day." And like all her siblings, she guessed that she was his favorite. Her saddest memory is being told about his brain tumor.

As the oldest grandchild, Kara was well positioned to observe a mature Mac, long after his political life was behind him. Kara remembers Mac's grandfatherly strengths—he was tireless, Christmas was his favorite holiday, his greatest accomplishment was "our Mom," he was a little vain. He used that wipe-on color when he went gray.

Kara spoke for all her siblings when she said "Mac's saddest day was when LBJ died, and his happiest was whenever we went to see him."

Mac's children and grandchildren. Wesley Bolin Memorial Plaza, McFarland Memorial dedication, 2015.

26

Mac and KTVK, 1971

F ew things ever awed Mac, but television was one of them. Mac is best known in American politics as the father of the GI Bill. What few people knew then, or now, is that Mac had two areas of expertise while in the Senate—veterans affairs and communications. World War II was one of the country's darkest times, second only to the Civil War. But the war years rapidly transformed technology. The year before Mac was elected to the Senate, Senator Burton K. Wheeler, a Democrat from Montana, chaired the Senate's Interstate Commerce Committee (ICC). Under his leadership, the committee began a study of the telegraph industry. That industry's importance was evident when war in Europe broke out in 1939. It was telegraphy, not television, that first attracted Mac's attention.

His work there and inside the ICC gave Mac the broad understanding of how important and how valuable communications was to everything that happened in America. As a first-term senator, Mac had the good fortune to be asked by Wheeler to become deeply involved with investigations and legislation concerning the nation's major telegraph companies, Western Union and Postal. Years later, Mac was invited to join Western Union's board of directors.

Both companies were vital to the war effort, and both were financially struggling. Mac chaired the 1942 investigating subcommittee. He called fifty-one witnesses before his committee and isolated one major cause for the decline in telephone, radio, teletype, and airmail operations across the country—technology. The underlying problem with expanding and acquiring new technology was the competition not only with one another, but also with communication systems in the U.S. Army and U.S. Navy. Mac favored the merging of Postal and Western Union, but he ran headfirst into Ohio Senator Robert A. Taft, known then as "Mr. Republican." Taft opposed the merger because it might favor labor. Mac's floor arguments prevailed, and the merger bill passed the Senate. Roosevelt signed the bill into law on March 6, 1943. That led to later legislative investigations and legislation in the film industry, postwar policies for international communications, freedom of the press, and free exchange of news.

Mac's argument was a signature piece in debates on the floor of the senate.

> The plain fact is that we have no policy adequately representing American interests in international communications. It is surprising and shocking to those who talk about the greatness of the United States, but there is no denial that a nation that is the richest, most powerful and greatest industrially and commercially, and thus most concerned with foreign trade, has been and is now a third-rate power in communications.

Mac immersed himself deep into communications barnstorming and all of the legal and technical consequences of national and international communications. McMillan's political masterpiece makes the connection between Mac's interest and expertise in communications and his advancement at the national level on policy at the highest levels.

One small feature of Mac's relationship with people led the fact that he became among the first in Washington to know of FDR's death in Warm Springs, Georgia, on April 12, 1945. As it happened, Mac was trying to make a call to Florida, but the telephone lines were tied up in preparation for the announcement of FDR's death. He crossed the congressional mall to what he called a social appointment with Speaker of the House Sam Rayburn and Vice-President

Harry Truman. That "social call" usually involved a drink or two. Mac walked into the Speaker's office at the same moment Vice-President Truman and Speaker Rayburn learned the president was dead. That misfortune shifted the currents of fate in Mac's career. He would very soon work much closer with, and earn more influence from President Truman.

Mac's abilities were quickly recognized at the national and international level. He became intimately involved in the ensuing investigations into communications in the European and Mediterranean theaters of war. Truman and Mac had been close associates from their Senate days and were becoming increasingly reliant upon each other as their careers progressed. They were a lot alike—homespun cloth, so to speak. They had adjacent desks during the Seventy-Seventh Congress. Both had rural, midwestern prairie upbringing. Both had World War I experience. Both were thirty-second-degree Freemasons. Both had engaged in legislative and judicial matters early in their careers. Mac worked with Truman on many issues, not the least of which were matters involving the Federal Communications Commission (FCC). Eventually, Mac's knowledge and experience on FCC matters paid off in the running of his television empire in Arizona.

In the mid-1970s, Mac set up all of his grandchildren with stock in the TV station he had started. Mac did this the way you'd expect from a doting grandfather who had instilled both good business practices and personal responsibility in his five grandchildren. He loaned them the money to buy shares of stock from him. The stock dividends were designated to pay taxes on stock transactions and pay Mac a modest-rate interest on his loan to them. Mac and his lawyers explained that the IRS code required this process.

Most of the grandchildren have unique memories of their experiences at KTVK. John Lewis remembers the day when he went to Mac's KTVK office for a visit. Mac said, "Come with me, John, we have a meeting with the bankers in the conference room." John was sixteen, lived in Florence on the farm, and had never met a banker. Mac introduced him to the bankers as "my grandson and a stockholder of this TV station."

The Valley Bank, Mac's first employer in Arizona in 1919, was now his lead bank in Arizona, and KTVK was a principal client. They apparently were not doing "a very good job investing the profit sharing program for the employees of the TV station. So, called them on the carpet for their performance." It was a lesson John never forgot.

When he left the Arizona Supreme Court in January 1971, Mac began consolidating his Channel 3 ownership solely in his family—the McFarland and Lewis families. In June of that year, he obtained approval from the FCC to buy out his nonfamily partners at Channel 3 for $5.91 million. He'd owned half the company since February 1955, when he obtained Arizona Television Company's first FCC license. At the outset, Mac made things clear—KTVK was chosen as the name "because TV will be our middle name." While it was always successful, KTVK still had its problems. Its new programming was second to KOOL TV, Channel 10.

When Mac died in 1984, his daughter, Jewell McFarland Lewis, inherited the station. She ran it alongside her husband, Del. Del and most of their children had worked at the station for years. By the late 1980s, KTVK was back on top as the top-rated television station in Arizona. Mac had run the station as a mom-and-pop operation, and the Lewis family continued that style—open doors and lots of hugs. But bad news struck in 1994 when New World Communications announced an affiliation deal with Fox in which twelve of its stations, including the CBS affiliate in Phoenix, KSAZ-TV, would defect from ABC and join Fox.

The Lewis family lost a challenge at the FCC, perhaps because Mac was no longer the player he once had been with the FCC. So Jewell and Del turned KTVK into an independent station. It owned a substantial programming inventory. The pressure to compete with major giant corporate affiliates was intense. MAC America sold most of its media assets, including KTVK in 1999, to the Belo Corporation, ending forty-four years of McFarland-Lewis ownership.

27

Mac's Memorial at the State Capitol, 1998 and 2015

The first official state memorial to Mac, dedicated in 1998, focused on Mac's work on veterans' benefits and water rights. But over time it deteriorated, and the state did little to maintain either its physical aspects or the legacy it represented. So, in 2013, with John Lewis in the lead, his grandchildren began a monumental effort to restore Mac's legacy and his place in American history. They spent $400,000 to rebuild the physical monument. They also established a fund for future repairs and maintenance. It was unveiled in 2015 on Arizona Statehood Day, February 14, at the state capital's Wesley Bolin Plaza.

Arizona Capital Times reporter Rachel Leingang captured the spirit and emotional connection between thousands of Arizonans and Mac. She revealed the tragedy Mac faced at a critical juncture in his life. Her physical description of the bricks-and-mortar part of the memorial is inspiring. The photo at the top of her article says it all. It depicts a stunning block of granite with the words, ERNEST W. MCFARLAND AND THE AMERICAN DREAM. She walks her readers through the path.

> The memorial's spiral path, flanked by panels telling about McFarland's life and accomplishments, end in a prominent 24-foot tall arch. About halfway

through the path a scar cuts through the concrete and marble memorial, a feature that demonstrates the loss of McFarland's first wife and children to disease. McFarland's personal loss coincided with the Great Depression.

Leingang interviewed the memorial's leader, John Lewis, and its architect, Don Ryden. Lewis said his grandfather had "worked so hard, and the old memorial was just disgusting to the family . . . now he has the memorial he deserves." Ryden knew designing a world-class memorial would be a challenge because "Mac was a great, but humble man who would have wanted no monument." He was right. Mac sought publicity only for the causes and needs of the American people. He shunned self-aggrandizement. True, he sought votes and reelection to high office, but not as a monument to himself. Ryden knew that because he told the reporter, "That's why this memorial ideally will inspire people to see parallels in their own lives and challenge them to achieve success despite adversity. This is meant to be an architectural fanfare to the common man."

Leingang's article directs visitors to the memorial to take close note of what happens when a visitor reaches the end of the spiral path; it's the signature feature of the memorial.

"At the end of the path, near the arch, a rock features a plaque that honors McFarland, but the photo on the rock won't show the former lawmaker's face. It shows a workhorse, intended to reveal and challenge those who visit the memorial," said the memorial's architect, Don Ryden. "It isn't achieving your dream that's the point. The prize is the legacy he left behind for everybody on the way," Ryden said.[1]

The memorial is unlike any other in Arizona because it creates a bond between the man it honors and many other things that make Arizonans proud. It sits beside Arizona's World War II memorial—wartime and sacrifice. Ryden explained, "The McFarland memorial exemplifies the postwar boom, with its asymmetrical, but balanced, and optimistic feel."

John Lewis knows that memorial like the back of his hand. He hopes that "visitors learn about his grandfather, and the kind of man he was, and that they're moved by his action by his journey. I'd like them to walk away from this kind of like seeing a really good movie that inspires you, and makes you think."

Epilogue, 2017

Biographies about famous people inevitably challenge authors who write decades after their subjects die. Richard Holmes, one of the world's most famous biographers, knew the challenge well.

Biography is the art of tracking the dead and fixing them on the printed page. The job is daunting—you have to establish an imaginary relationship with a non-existent person, or at least a dead one.

Unlike fiction, biography always brings the author face-to-face with a literary crevasse when existing documentation fails to reveal the facts of a man's life. In Mac's case, Arizona state archivists, with help from Vince Murray, McFarland staff, and family members, took on the monumental task of gathering, organizing, archiving, and preserving his written, photographic, and digital record. The job took years, and parts of that record have yet to be properly archived. Nonetheless, the existing record is a stack of cardboard boxes, which if placed side by side would run between two hundred and three hundred linear feet. It is housed in various museums, historical archives, university libraries, family garages, and storerooms.

Mac's political life from 1940 to 1971 was never a literary crevasse for McMillan, Mac's principal biographer. McMillan encapsulated the political record in one massive 2004 volume. But this 2018 book tells Mac's Arizona story while incorporating context from Mac's senatorial career. True stories like this one are neither memoir or historical prose. Mac's own autobiography was not memoir, but rather a factual presentation of Mac's own historical record. But neither McMillan's political biography nor Mac's autobiography was written to tell, in narrative prose, the story behind the facts or the emotional aspects of tragedy and setback, which were very much a part of Mac's life.

Hopefully, this book is not just a long-form, book-length obituary. A man's story written by someone other than himself opens the literary possibility that the man is not necessarily dead. Mac's Arizona story *still* lives, while his political story is the stuff of history books. It was important to bring Mac back, alive and well, once again on these pages, telling *his* story seventy-seven years after he lived it.

Holmes also said, "The dead are immortal, the more so if you acknowledge the essential open-endedness of the exercise."

Virginia Woolf, an English author in the interwar period, "slyly observed that the actual length of a person's life is open to dispute. Lives don't necessarily end on deathbeds." They sometimes are told in biographies, and so live on the page you're reading. People read biographies out of curiosity, sometimes passionately so. The reader cannot know how the story ends because it never does.

Mac's story about spending World War I in sick bay at a naval hospital is missing from his own autobiography. His story about loving Clare and losing their children is absent from his 1979 penmanship. His political story is carefully woven over and around the details inherent in his personal challenges as though they didn't exist. And people who knew him well, albeit long after he rose above his grief, still have little understanding of how he felt, how often he cried out in the dark of night, and whether he almost gave up or in.

But history is its own teacher. Family history, which, by its very nature, is rarely reduced to writing, doesn't die any more than a Virginia Woolf character does, based on someone who once lived. Mac's son-in-law, Del Lewis Sr., likely knows how hard the loss of successive children and his first wife hit Mac. "I don't know how many people could recover from such personal events," Lewis said. "Somehow Mac did, and came back to achieve great things in his political life."

Vince Murray also saw that tragedy as the turning point in Mac's life. "I think that's what drove Mac when his early success was derailed. His efforts were no longer just about him, but what he could do for his community, his state and his country."

Mac's written record confirms what was always there in plain sight, but never reduced to prose. It was the "essential" Mac, the Mac no one knew but everyone loved. The Mac who rarely talked about his family in public settings, while on the job, or as part of a political campaign. The Mac who suffered in silence the personal tragedies in 1919 and 1930. His archival record is silent about the new life he found with Edna and Jewell in 1939. Mac suffered his losses in private but his gains in the newspapers. That's what gave him the strength to go on. Mac's written record, precisely because it says so little about his family life, is silent testimony about how careful he was to protect his family from the glare of public life. By its absence, his family life is walled off from and protected against his rough-and-tumble professional life. That singular characteristic, tamping down the tragic and ramping up public service, is vital to this book.

He carefully constructed the public record of his achievements. It is there for all to see. He worked the public trough day in and day out and articulated all of it in plain *Mac* speak. He was not a vain man, but he wanted to be noticed. He wasn't boastful, but he was justifiably proud of how he helped family, friends, clients, litigants, and constituents. The private family record remains private, just like he wanted it. In digging down past the obvious sources in public archives, I struggled to find the emotional story of Mac's loss and gain in the thirties. I never found it. But the effort alone told me why I didn't find it.

Mac was never lyrical, never given to metaphor in either his public life or his private one. But had he been so inclined, the metaphor that comes to mind, when thinking about his story, is the Gila River. In Mac's early adulthood, it was an important and, on occasion, raging river on the north side of Florence. Today it is, charitably, a dry gulch, except during the rare torrential rain that hits that part of Arizona. The once beautiful Gila River banks bore witness to Mac's unknown story of the pain of losing Clare and their children. It knew about Mac falling in love with Edna and how important young Jewell was to his life. And, like all rivers, it sheltered and comforted the people of Florence while keeping the secrets of everyone who stopped by.

The passage of seventy-seven years is an insurmountable barrier. But now, even if I had access to Mac's love letters or the emotional recollections of his closest friends, there would be little that revealed private things that Mac *wanted* kept private. Had I been able to somehow peek into the new life Mac started with Edna, I'd have seen nothing. The best and the worst of Mac's family life were family matters, never to be confused with public matters. There were backyards and watering tanks all over that part of Pinal County on both banks of the Gila. Everyone there knew about the tragedies in the McFarland family. But there is no written record about Mac's losses, his feelings, or how he grieved. That doesn't mean his friends didn't grieve for him or talk about the family in private. It just means they honored Mac by not talking about him in public.

What I learned from my search for Mac's feelings is that it really doesn't matter so much where you begin the story of a famous man or even where it ends. What matters is that you write until you get back to your starting point. I could not find Mac's feelings about loss or how thrilled he was about gain, precisely because he didn't want me to know. To quote Colette, "To attempt achievement is to come back to one's starting point."

There's a famous story about Friedrich Nietzsche and how he dealt with loss and rejection. Forlorn and dejected, he'd gone to London to pick up a rejected manuscript from a publisher. Riding the train back home, he held the bulky bundle on his lap, facedown. As London faded away behind him, he began a new book on the back pages of the rejected one. That's what Mac did. His first narrative was Clare, and he loved her dearly. But when he lost her, instead of commiserating, he bided his time. Edna came into his life. Mac knew something that many people in tragic circumstances never fully accept. He lost Ernest Jr., Jean Clare, and Juliet, but he gained Jewell. He started over by coming back to his starting point. In his case, it was finding the right woman to live the life he wanted to live. He never considered going it alone.

It was no accident that Mac met and married two high school teachers. His own first start after college in Oklahoma was teaching. After graduating from East Central State Teachers College in Ada, Oklahoma, he took on his first full-time job off the family farm. That country-school experience was his first professional challenge. He taught in a small, rural school ruled by husky farm boys; they nearly undid the calm, gentle lad from Earlsboro. The two teachers who'd preceded him at that school were forced to leave because they couldn't cope with their charges. But Mac proved he was the boss in the classroom the same way he'd proved his worth on the farm. He was not only well prepared, he was tough. His classroom was marked by "serenity and discipline." He loved children, whether in that one-room school in Oklahoma, or in his first adobe home in Florence, with Clare and their babies. That love came back to him when Edna came into his life, with her ten-year-old daughter, Jewell. She turned out to be what Mac had always hoped for—a daughter with his brains, his wife's beauty and composure, and a willingness to stick with him, through trials, wonderful times, and a few tribulations.

Mac died at eighty-nine in 1984 with more official accolades, more years of service rendered, and more political achievement that any other Arizonan. He died with immeasurable universal respect from every state and every part of the American population. Parts of Europe mourned as well because he was known there and had mingled happily and with honest sincerity there. Arizona celebrated its seventy-second anniversary of statehood that year. Mac's surviving contemporaries cherished his friendship. Arizona's political, professional, business, and agricultural communities sighed and commiserated with his extended family. Many mourners were men and women of national and international fame.

In modesty, generosity, and devotion to the rule of law, Mac excelled in ways few others did. He had a scrupulous regard for honor in public and private affairs. His stoic self-restraint made him nearly a faultless representative of his birth state, Oklahoma, and his adopted state, Arizona. America owes him an enormous debt for the remarkable way he went about becoming the man everyone knew as Mac.

In reviewing his unparalleled political feat—elected prosecutor, elected judge, elected senator, elected majority leader, elected governor, elected Arizona Supreme Court chief justice—it is almost impossible to believe that he accomplished all of that with his sterling reputation intact. Historian Vince Murray, who studied Mac's life and has helped the McFarland/Lewis family advance Mac's legacy for many years, explained how Mac did that.

"Pretty much everyone on both sides of the aisle liked him, even if they disagreed with him. He was noted by his political colleagues as being courteous, fair and impartial, and for his spirit of cooperation."

Dr. Jack August, a noted author and Arizona's official historian, knew Mac well. He offered an insider's view into how Mac worked in our national legislature. "I think his post-World War I struggles, when he barely made it out alive and lacked veteran's benefits, shaped his attitude toward helping returning servicemen during World War II."

This book is about how and why everyone who knew Prosecutor McFarland and Judge McFarland felt at ease in just calling him "Mac." That elemental phrase, "call me Mac," reveals what everyone knew about him—he wasn't for show, he was for real. But once Mac reached the rarified air in Washington, DC, he could have changed—he could have insisted on rigorous adherence to formality. He could have swallowed and savored that famous political snobbery that dominated the elite and powerful in American government. After all, Mac was no longer just another farmer with a law degree from casual Arizona. He'd moved up onto the national political stage in Washington, DC. But as we all know now, Mac never moved up—he was Mac here, there, and everywhere.

Esquire magazine profiled him in 1942—they called him "presidential material." The editorial staff discovered little things that might not have been common in Washington but were well known in Arizona.

"His sharp mind and work ethic, fueled by a daily dose of 20 cups of black coffee, inspired the label 'prime presidential material.' According to his staff, he'd be at his Senate office until late in the evening, long after the 9-to-5 people had gone home." That June 1942 coverage was one of Mac's first forays into national media. That edition highlighted "Esky Gambling at Training Camp" on its cover, but Mac's profile was the lead story. There were many short articles, including one about English Springer Spaniels and a homey little piece titled "Adjusting Your Nerves to War." Gypsy Rose Lee wrote an *Esquire* special titled "War Isn't Sport." *Esquire* featured a Varga foldout, and the most frequently viewed page was the Jane Russell pinup foldout. Mac knew GIs everywhere would love that. That would stick with troops; they wouldn't spend much time reading about him, he likely assumed. But two years later, every veteran in America, including those in combat across two oceans, got the GI Bill. They stilled loved Jane Russell, but what Mac gave them was better than a look; it was their ticket to a better life.

By his second senatorial term, Mac knew presidential talent when he saw it. That's why he tapped Lyndon Baines Johnson as his whip when he was elected to serve as majority leader in 1951. The political aspirations of the McFarland-Johnson team were as high as the moon in 1951. But all of it was sequestered under Dwight David Eisenhower's political avalanche in 1952.

Massachusetts Senator Henry Cabot Lodge Jr. was close to Mac even though they were in opposing political parties. In 1951, he began an Eisenhower for President drive in the Republican Party. It's fair to assume that Senator Lodge did not give much thought to what his efforts might do to Mac's own electoral future. In public, Eisenhower had dismissed any political interests because he was commander of NATO forces in Europe. But behind the scenes, Eisenhower began to offer encouragement to Lodge during the senator's visits to NATO headquarters near Paris. Finally, in January 1952, Eisenhower announced that he was a Republican and would be willing to accept the call of the American people to serve as president.

Mac's party, the Democrats, picked Governor Adlai Stevenson of Illinois, a witty and urbane politician whose thoughtful speeches appealed to both liberals and moderate Democrats. His credentials were impressive: he was a Princeton-educated lawyer who had served as special assistant to the secretary of the navy during World War II, an influential member of the U.S. delegation to the United Nations after the war, and a successful governor with an enviable record of reform. But as a campaigner, he was no match for Eisenhower, just as Henry Fountain Ashurst had proved he was no match for Mac.

Had you been watching Eisenhower's campaign, you might have thought he sounded a lot like Mac: confident, a plain talker, always with a reassuring smile. Mac was also a veteran, albeit nowhere close to Eisenhower, the greatest military leader in American history. Very much like Mac, Eisenhower kept a demanding schedule, traveling to forty-five states and speaking to large crowds from the caboose of his campaign train. The slogan *I like Ike* quickly became part of the political language of America. On election day, Eisenhower won big—with 55 percent of the popular vote and a landslide in the electoral college. The final tally was 442 votes to Stevenson's 89.

Even so, Eisenhower's coattails did not carry many Republicans into Congress. The GOP won control of Congress but only by narrow majorities—three seats in the House of Representatives, one seat in the Senate. *One* seat. *Mac's* seat. When Mac died in 1984, even Goldwater praised him.

> I voted for Mac once, as a Republican. I would have voted for him again, but it would have meant voting against me.

Mac's personal story can never be separated from his political life, regardless of how hard he tried to keep the political world away from his family. If nothing else, his lifetime request that everyone just call him Mac is as personal as it was political. There was no anticipation that he'd lead America as majority leader after World War II. Nothing that happened in plain sight from the day in 1919 when he arrived in Arizona to the day he took the senatorial oath of office in 1941 could have predicted his provenance as one of America's great leaders and as Arizona's favorite son.

"This is a Senate of equals," Daniel Webster explained in 1830. "We know no masters, we acknowledge no dictators," he said. Since it first convened in 1789, nearly two thousand individuals have served in the U.S. Senate, each bringing his or her own special talents and qualities to the office. But Mac was one of only twelve Arizonans to serve in the U.S. Senate from statehood to now and the only one to be elected majority leader by his colleagues. Arizona has had only twenty-two governors—Mac was one of them. Twenty-one men and two women served as chief justices on the Arizona Supreme Court. Mac was also one of them.

No other American has even tried to match Mac's final act. However, distinguished they were, they all retired after their public service was done. Mac didn't. At seventy-one, he owned and led a very large commercial enterprise. At eighty-four, he died a multimillionaire. That wasn't a Triple Crown, a Final Four, a Superbowl, or being elected to the Rock and Roll Hall of Fame; it was just plain old Mac doing in his seventies what he'd done in his twenties.

Mac's most important service to Arizona and the United States was his service as majority leader in the U.S. Senate from 1951 to 1953. He was the seventh man to serve as majority leader and only one of nineteen in American history. If the Senate is in fact "America's Most Exclusive Club," then its majority leaders are the epitome of exclusiveness. Only one Arizonan ever rose to that level—Mac—and no one could have predicted it. Mac chose his deputy, the whip, carefully. He chose the man who ultimately became known as "Master of the Senate," before he became president of the United States, Lyndon B. Johnson. Thirty-seven of the fifty states have yet to send a citizen to the U.S. Senate and rise to election as majority leader. While his senatorial accomplishments were many, clearly his signature legislation was the GI Bill, which helped millions of veterans get a college education. I know that because I was one of them.

If Mac were a character in a novel, he would be urbane and influential but still a farmer at heart. He would be highly educated but welcome company in a working-class cafe. He would be a man of conventional midwestern upbringing but with a never-quenched appetite for life in the desert. While educated in the classics and the law, he would shine most brightly in his postgraduate study of political science. And most importantly, he would be portrayed with homespun personality and an engaging smile. He would be available to and a champion of the common men and women of America.

At the party in January 1980 to introduce his autobiography, many famous Arizonans paid tribute. Former Arizona governor Bruce Babbitt called Mac's career "a metaphor for what has taken place in Arizona." Babbitt told the large crowd of friends, family, and admirers at the McFarland State Park in Florence that Mac reminded him of "John Quincy Adams, who after serving as U.S. President, returned home and served his home state as a representative to Congress. Both were motivated by the same thing."

"Because he felt he was put on this earth to serve, Mac did that again and again," said Governor Rose Mofford, one of Mac's closest friends. She traced Mac's ownership of KTVK, *after* serving the state as assistant attorney general, Pinal County prosecutor, Pinal County judge, U.S. senator, majority leader, Arizona governor, and Arizona Supreme Court chief justice.

Mac got two standing ovations at that signing party and saved his closing remarks for his wife. He said, "There was one person who stood by me throughout all of it. I couldn't have done it without her. Edna McFarland."

In today's parlance, Edna and Jewell were a package deal. Mac adopted Jewell just after he married her mother. He became the first man, important or otherwise, in her life. To say they doted on one another is an understatement. Jewell was seven when Mac began courting her mother. That was the same year she met a boy who also lived in Florence, Del Lewis—he was eleven. Eventually, Jewell would marry Del, but first she learned what the world was all about from her stepfather. Not long after Jewell moved with her mom and Mac to Washington, DC, Del joined the navy, like her stepfather. Del served in the Pacific theater during World War II, while his future wife went to school in DC. When the war ended, Del came home to his parent's farm in Florence about the same time Jewell came home to Mac's farm in Florence. They entered the University of Arizona together, dated for four years, and graduated together in 1951. They wanted to marry immediately upon graduation, but Jewell had promised Mac she'd get her master's degree in education in Washington before she married. As soon as she did, she got married.

Dell had been working as a civil engineer for the Army Corps of Engineers in Virginia. Once married, Mac gave them a new opportunity. They could move back to Florence. Del would assume responsibility for the McFarland farms near Florence and Casa Grande, and Jewell could set up remedial reading programs in Florence and Coolidge. Meanwhile, she would enter the PhD program in education from at Arizona State College. She earned that PhD about the time her college became Arizona State University.

Finis Mac

Mac's story began on page one. It ends here. Because there was only one Mac and only one life born again on these pages, it seems fitting to end where his story began. This book was about a teacher, lawyer, judge, and a senator, too. A governor, supreme court justice, and an entrepreneur, too. An author, husband, father, grandfather, and a great-grandfather, too. Turns out, it's not just his story. It belongs in unequal shares to Clare, Ernest Jr., Jean Clare, Juliet, Edna, Jewell, Kara, Bill, John, Leah, Dell Jr., and seven great-grandchildren whose stories have not yet been written. There are lesser characters, too, and calling them that is no slur. Henry Fountain Ashurst, Tom Fulbright, Irving A. Jennings, Franklin Delano Roosevelt, Harry Truman, George Marshall, Carl Hayden, Barry Goldwater, and the thousands of politicians, lawyers, farmers, judges, clients, colleagues, opponents, constituents, and those who followed his path are part of his story, too. And he was, as lawyers would say, *sui generis*. One of a kind.

If Mac could read this, he'd likely remind every reader to remember just one thing: "Call me Mac, everybody does." And now you know why the title of this book is *Call Him Mac*.

Acknowledgments

Thanks to Kara Lewis, Bill Lewis, John Lewis, Leah Lewis, and Dell Lewis Jr., for their confidence in me and for giving the rest of Arizona the opportunity to know more about Mac, its favorite son. Thanks to Fritz Aspey for thinking of me and helping the Lewis clan to advance Mac's legacy. Thanks to the staff at the Sandra Day O'Connor College of Law Library for their help in uncovering the story. Thanks to the researchers and archivists at the Polly Rosenbloom State Library and Archives for their patience and never-ending supply of cardboard boxes about Mac. Thanks to the people of Pinal County, and especially Florence, for their memories and stories about Mac. Special thanks to the McFarland Historical State Park staff for allowing me to muse at will through the rooms and hallways in Florence and for trying to find answers to my unanswerable questions. Most of all, I must thank, posthumously, a fine historian, Dr. James E. McMillan. He dug deeply for decades into Mac's political life. The massive record in his manuscript made my job much simpler. I spent the better part of a day in December 2004 with him, talking about books, history, and Arizona. Neither of us knew then that I'd write this book or that I'd find his book so helpful. Jim is no longer with us, but he lives on in my book, just as Mac lived on in his book.

And as is always the case, thanks to my wife, Kathleen Stuart, for doing what she always does. She reads my first draft, and then makes me write it again, without all those mistakes.

Notes

Mac: Sooner Born and Sooner Bred, 1894

1. Wayne Morgan and Anne Hodges Morgan, *Oklahoma: A History* (New York: W. W. Norton & Co., 1977), 51. This passage and other aspects of life in Oklahoma are more fully reported in James E. McMillan, "First Sooner Senator: Ernest W. McFarland's Oklahoma Years, 1894–1919," *Chronicles of Oklahoma* 72 (Summer 1994): 178–99.
2. McMillan, "First Sooner Senator," 6.
3. McMillan, "First Sooner Senator." See also John A. Walker, ed., *The East Central [Oklahoma] Story: From Normal School to University* (Ada, Okla.: East Central University, 1984).
4. The textbooks are in MP, series 7, box 295.
5. Anne Hodges Morgan, *Robert S. Kerr: The Senate Years* (Norman: University of Oklahoma Press, 1977).
6. Pesagi, East Central Normal School Yearbook 1915. Located in MP, series 7, box 295.
7. Ernest W. McFarland, *Mac: The Autobiography of Ernest W. McFarland* (Phoenix, Ariz.: n.p., 1979), 13–15.
8. Briles had backed the wrong man for governor of Oklahoma in the 1914 primaries. The new Oklahoma governor, Robert L. Williams, targeted Briles for removal as college president. His case was tried in state court in Ada,

Oklahoma, in June 1915. He was acquitted of all charges, but his professional stature was permanently damaged, and he was dismissed a year later in the summer of 1916. James McMillan, *Ernest W. McFarland: Majority Leader of the United States Senate, Governor and Chief Justice of the State of Arizona* (Sharlot Hall Museum Press, 2006), 14.

9. McFarland, *Mac: The Autobiography*, 15–16.
10. McFarland, *Mac: The Autobiography*, 16.
11. *The Sooner*, University of Oklahoma (1917), 83. MP, series 7, box 295.

Mac Joins the U.S. Navy, 1917

1. Keziah McFarland Collection. MP series 8, subseries 1, box 298, 6–7.
2. See Robert Wesley Angelo, "The Influenza Pandemic of 1918," ROAngelo.net, last modified January 4, 2009, accessed March 24, 2018, http://www.roangelo.net/schlectweg/influenz.html.
3. The U.S. Navy rank of commander, officer pay grade 0-5, is the same as lieutenant colonel in the U.S. Marine Corps.
4. McFarland, *Mac: The Autobiography*, 25.

Mac: Law, Political Science, and Sociology, 1919

1. McMillan, *Ernest W. McFarland*, 22. Materials about Mac's Stanford years are in MP, box 296.
2. McMillan, *Ernest W. McFarland*, 22, n. 6.
3. McMillan, *Ernest W. McFarland*, 24.
4. McMillan, *Ernest W. McFarland*, 28, n. 1. MP box 284; E. W. McFarland, "The Operation of the Initiative and Referendum in California," master's thesis, Stanford University, 1924.

Mac and Florence, Arizona, 1924

1. Journals of the Eighth Legislative Assembly of the Territory of Arizona (Tucson Office of the Arizona Citizen), 1875; James M. Murphy, *Laws, Courts, and Lawyers Through the Years in Arizona* (Tucson: University of Arizona Press, 1970), chap. 10.
2. Murphy, *Laws, Courts, and Lawyers*, 148.
3. Murphy, *Laws, Courts, and Lawyers*, 149.
4. McMillan, *Ernest W. McFarland*, 47.
5. McFarland, *Mac: The Autobiography*, 30.
6. McMillan, *Ernest W. McFarland*, 31.

7. McMillan, *Ernest W. McFarland*, 32.
8. McMillan, *Ernest W. McFarland*, 48–49.
9. McMillan, *Ernest W. McFarland*, 41.
10. McMillan, *Ernest W. McFarland*, 41.

Mac Becomes a Lawyer, 1921

1. McFarland, *Mac: The Autobiography*, 27.
2. McFarland, *Mac: The Autobiography*, 38.
3. Murphy, *Laws, Courts, and Lawyers*. Murphy, a native Arizonan, graduated from the University of Arizona Law School, served as president of the Pima County Bar, the State Bar of Arizona, and as a member of the House of Delegates of the American Bar Association. He was an FBI agent in the 1940s and served as a lieutenant in the U.S. Navy during World War II. Murphy mentions Mac six times in his book about Arizona lawyers.
4. Murphy, *Laws, Courts, and Lawyers*, 104.
5. Murphy, *Laws, Courts, and Lawyers*, 104–105.
6. Murphy, *Laws, Courts, and Lawyers*, 106.
7. McFarland, *Mac: The Autobiography*, 28.
8. McMillan, *Ernest W. McFarland*, 23.
9. McMillan, *Ernest W. McFarland*, 23.
10. Ernest W. McFarland Papers, McFarland Historical State Park Library and Archives, MP, box 298.
11. *Session Laws, State of Arizona, 1925, Seventh Legislature, Regular Session*, chapters 2, 32, subdivision 7.
12. Murphy, *Laws, Courts, and Lawyers*, 109.
13. McFarland, *Mac: The Autobiography*, 29.

Mac Runs for Pinal County Attorney, 1924

1. Murphy, *Laws, Courts, and Lawyers*, 124.
2. Murphy, *Laws, Courts, and Lawyers*, 148.
3. McMillan, *Ernest W. McFarland*, 30.

Mac and Tommy Fulbright, 1929

1. Tom Fulbright, *Cow-Country Counselor* (Jericho, NY: Exposition Press, Inc., 1968).
2. The foreword was written by Allan K. Perry, another prominent member of the Arizona Bar Association. Perry was admitted to the bar with Tommy Fulbright, on January 1, 1932.

3. Fulbright, *Cow-Country Counselor*, 18.

Mac and the Eva Dugan Case, 1930

1. *Almgill v. Pierson*, 2 Bros. & Pull. (1797), 104.
2. Paul Allen, *Tucson Citizen*, October 29, 2005, 5A.
3. *Dugan v. State of Arizona*, 36 Ariz. 36, (1929) 39.
4. *Dugan v. State of Arizona*, 42.
5. McFarland, *Mac: The Autobiography*, 32.
6. McFarland, *Mac: The Autobiography*, 32.
7. McFarland, *Mac: The Autobiography*, 32.

Mac, Clare, and Their Children, 1925 to 1929

1. McMillan, *Ernest W. McFarland*, 33, n. 18.
2. Arizona State Archives, MG 98, series 8; family records, box 294–8.
3. McMillan, *Ernest W. McFarland*, 35.
4. McFarland, *Mac: The Autobiography*, 35.
5. McMillan, *Ernest W. McFarland*, 38, n. 23–24.
6. McMillan, *Ernest W. McFarland*, 34–35, n. 20.

Mac and Henry Fountain Ashurst in the 1930s

1. Bruce Bliven, *The New Republic*, December 11, 1935.
2. "Ashurst, Defeated, Reviews Service," *New York Times*, September 12, 1940, 18.
3. R. D. Lusk, "The Life and Death of 470 Acres," *Saturday Evening Post*, August 13, 1938.
4. Frederick Lewis Allen, "When the Farms Blew Away," in *The Thirties: A Time to Remember*, ed. Don Congdon (New York: Simon & Schuster, 1962), 386–90.
5. America's role as the unquestioned leader of the world's democracies may be facing a challenge as a consequence of the 2016 presidential elections. If the Trump administration advances a nationalist strategy that pays scant attention to settled and certain foreign policy positions at odds with all prior administrations, this position could change.
6. James MacGregor Burns, *Roosevelt: The Lion and the Fox* (Orlando, Fla.: Harcourt, Inc., 1956).
7. "Who's in the Army Now?" *Fortune* magazine, October 1935.
8. Dexter Perkins, *The New Age of Franklin Roosevelt* (Chicago: University of Chicago Press, 1957).

Mac and the Winnie Ruth Judd Case, 1934

1. There were no executions in Arizona between 1962 and 1992. Since then, prisoners have had their choice—lethal gas or lethal injection. Once legal injection became the death of choice (and law), fourteen inmates have been executed by lethal injection. None have been beheaded.
2. In the Matter of Winnie Ruth Judd, an Alleged Insane Person, Pinal County Superior Court Docket no. 1438, filed by T. J. Marks, clerk of the court.
3. McFarland, *Mac: The Autobiography*, 34.
4. McFarland, *Mac: The Autobiography*, 34.
5. McFarland, *Mac: The Autobiography*, 34–35.
6. McMillan, *Ernest W. McFarland*, 46, n. 6.

Mac Runs for Pinal County Judge Twice, 1930 and 1934

1. McMillan, *Ernest W. McFarland*, 37.
2. William E. Leuchtenburg, *Franklin D. Roosevelt and the New Deal, 1932–1940* (New York: Harper Perennial, 1963), 116–17.
3. McMillan, *Ernest W. McFarland*, 49, n. 10.
4. McMillan, *Ernest W. McFarland*, 38.
5. McMillan, *Ernest W. McFarland*, 39.

Mac's Primary Campaign Against Henry Fountain Ashurst, 1940

1. McMillan, *Ernest W. McFarland*, 41.
2. McFarland, *Mac: The Autobiography*, 42.
3. McFarland, *Mac: The Autobiography*, 44.
4. *Time* magazine, vol. 6, August 7, 1939.
5. Wikipedia, s.v. "Henry F. Ashurst," last modified February 8, 2018, 01:01, https://en.wikipedia.org/wiki/Henry_F._Ashurst.
6. McFarland, *Mac: The Autobiography*, 44.
7. McMillan, *Ernest W. McFarland*, 54.
8. McMillan, *Ernest W. McFarland*, 54.
9. McMillan, *Ernest W. McFarland*, 57.
10. McMillan, *Ernest W. McFarland*, 55, n. 20.
11. McMillan, *Ernest W. McFarland*, 55, n. 21.
12. McMillan, *Ernest W. McFarland*, 56, n. 22.
13. McMillan, *Ernest W. McFarland*, 59, n. 29; *The Messenger*, June 15, 1940, MP, series 1, box 1, *Arizona Republic*, August 31, 1940.
14. McMillan, *Ernest W. McFarland*, 59, n. 30.

15. McMillan, *Ernest W. McFarland*, 59, n. 31.
16. McMillan, *Ernest W. McFarland*, 50, n. 33.

Mac's Retail Politics, 1940

1. I practiced law with Mr. Jennings, Mr. Riggins at Jennings, Strouss and Salmon, and a few hundred other lawyers from 1966 to 1998.

Mac's General Election Campaign for the U.S. Senate, 1940

1. McMillan, *Ernest W. McFarland*, 51.
2. Arizona State Archives, McFarland Collection.
3. Don Congdon, ed., *The Thirties: A Time to Remember* (New York: Simon & Schuster, 1962).
4. 53 Ariz. 374, 89 P.2d 1060 (May 1, 1939).
5. Richard W. Steele, *Free Speech in the Good War* (New York: St. Martin's Press, 1999), 75–76.
6. Delbert Clark, "Aliens to Begin Registering Today," *New York Times*, August 25, 1940.

Mac, 1954 to 1964

1. Robert Sobel and John W. Raimo, *Biographical Directory of the Governors of the United States, 1789–1978*, vol. 1 (Westport, Conn.: Meckler Books, 1978).
2. *Arizona v. California*, 350 U.S. 114 (1955).

Mac's Grandchildren

1. The foundation is officially known as the McFarland Historical Park Advisory Committee, Inc., an Arizona nonprofit corporation.

Mac's Memorial at the State Capitol, 1998 and 2015

1. Rachel Leingang, "Memorial Honoring Ernest McFarland to Be Unveiled on Statehood Day," *Arizona Capitol Times*, February 13, 2015, https://azcapitoltimes.com/news/2015/02/13/memorial-honoring-ernest-mcfarland-to-be-unveiled-on-statehood-day/.

Bibliography

Allen, Frederick Lewis. "When the Farms Blew Away." In *The Thirties: A Time to Remember*, ed. Don Congdon, 386–90. New York: Simon & Schuster, 1962.

Arizona Recollections and Reflections, "Jewell McFarland Lewis and Del Lewis, Historymakers," *An Arizona Centennial Historymakers Commemoration, 1997*. Phoenix, Ariz.: Historical League, Inc., 2011, 168–71.

Baldwin, Ava S. "The History of Florence, Arizona," master's thesis, University of Arizona, 1941.

Bommersbach, Jana. *The Trunk Murderess, Winnie Ruth Judd: The Truth About an American Crime Legend Revealed at Last*. New York: Simon & Schuster, 1992.

Burns, James MacGregor. *Roosevelt: The Lion and the Fox*. Orlando, Fla.: Harcourt, Inc., 1956.

Congdon, Don, ed. *The Thirties: A Time to Remember*. New York: Simon & Schuster, 1962.

Ernest W. McFarland Papers. McFarland Historical State Park Library and Archives, Florence, Ariz.

Flood, John. *McFarland Landmark Cases*. McFarland State Park Archives: Florence, Ariz., n.d.

Fulbright, Tom. *Cow-Country Counselor*. Jericho, N.Y.: Exposition Press, Inc., 1968.

Henry F. Ashurst Papers, University of Arizona Libraries Special Collections, Tucson, Ariz.

Leuchtenburg, William. *Franklin D. Roosevelt and the New Deal*. New York: Harper Perennial, 1963.

McFarland, Ernest W. *Mac: The Autobiography of Ernest W. McFarland.* Phoenix, Ariz.: n.p., 1979.

———. "The Operation of the Initiative and Referendum in California," master's thesis. Stanford University, 1924.

McMillan, James E. "Father of the GI Bill: Ernest W. McFarland and Veterans Legislation," *Journal of Arizona History* 35, no. 4 (Winter 1994): 357.

McMillan, James E. "First Sooner Senator: Ernest W. McFarland's Oklahoma Years, 1894–1919," *Chronicles of Oklahoma* 72 (Summer 1994): 178–99.

McMillan, James Elton, Jr. *Ernest W. McFarland: Majority Leader of the United States Senate, Governor and Chief Justice of the State of Arizona.* Florence, Ariz.: Ernest W. McFarland Foundation, 2004.

———, ed. *The Ernest W. McFarland Papers: The United States Senate Years, 1940–1952.* Prescott, Ariz.: Sharlot Hall Museum Press, 1995.

Morgan, Anne Hodges. *Robert S. Kerr: The Senate Years.* Norman: University of Oklahoma Press, 1977.

Morgan, Wayne, and Anne Hodges Morgan. *Oklahoma: A History.* New York: W. W. Norton & Co., 1977.

Murphy, James M. *Laws, Courts, and Lawyers Through the Years in Arizona.* Tucson: University of Arizona Press, 1970.

Perkins, Dexter. *The New Age of Franklin Roosevelt.* Chicago: University of Chicago Press, 1957.

Pinal County Historical Society, *Florence, Arizona*, Images of America. Charleston, S.C.: Arcadia Publishing, 2007.

Sobel, Robert, and John W. Raimo. *Biographical Directory of the Governors of the United States, 1789–1978*, vol. 1. Westport, Conn.: Meckler Books, 1978.

Steele, Richard W. *Free Speech in the Good War.* New York: St. Martin's Press, 1999.

Stuart, Gary L. *Miranda: The Story of America's Right to Remain Silent.* Tucson: University of Arizona Press, 2004.

Walker, John A., ed. *The East Central [Oklahoma] Story: From Normal School to University.* Ada, Okla.: East Central University, 1984.

Index

Acheson, Dean, 151–52
Ackerman, Vernon, 47–49
Allen, Paul, 50
Arizona: counties of, 38; death penalty and, 54–55, 73, 77–78; as a Democratic state, 154; early history of, 19–20, 27, 38; economy of, 31; exploration of, 27; farming and, 31, 85, 113–14, 126, 130–31; The Great Depression and, 31; irrigation and, 114, 130–31; legal history of, 33–37; mining and, 27, 31, 115–16; water law and, 85, 114, 130–32
Arizona Bar Association, 33–37, 41, 91, 108
Arizona Capital Times, 181–82
Arizona Republic, 139–44, 153, 167
Arizona State Parks System, 156
Arizona State Prison, 28, 73
Arizona Supreme Court, 29, 35–37, 77, 84–85, 160–67, 180
Arnold, Ben, 173–74
Ashurst, Henry Fountain: 1940 Democratic Senate primary and, 93–97, 99–104; early history of, 90–91; education of, 90–91, 97; E.H. Duffield and, 92–96; Ernest William McFarland and, 93–97, 99–104; isolationism of, 92–93, 95; law school and, 91–92, 97; patriotism of, 93–95; perceptions of, 98–101; physical description of, 92; political career of, 92; private practive and, 91–92; prohibition and, 101; Senate committees and, 102; as a senator, 98–99; as a sheriff, 98; tariffs and, 101; water law and, 119
Ashurst-Hayden Dam, 29–30
AT&T, 70, 129
August, Jack, 188

Babbitt, Bruce, 191
Bailey, Weldon J., 35–36
Baker, Sam, 46–47
Barkley, Alben, 146–47
Barnum, Tom, 19
Bernstein, Charles, 164
Bibolet, Ronald, 154

Bommersbach, Jana, 74, 76
Branaman, Harris, 48–49
Branaman, Steve, 48–49
Branch, Bernard, 103
Bugg, John J., 116
Burden, Jack, 119–20
Butterfield, Lee, 48–49

Casa Grande, 27, 34, 39, 45–46, 99, 192
Central Arizona Project, 159
Chapman, Joe, 48–49
Chavez, Dennis, 146
Chenowth, John A., 19
Civilian Conservation Corps, 132–33
Clark, John P., 109
Clingan, Burt H., 125
Coker, Elmer, 49
Colorado River, 29, 111, 114, 119
Colorado River Boundary Commission, 156
Colorado River Compact, 131
communism, 133
conscription, 102–3, 120–21, 135–36
Coolidge, Calvin, 30, 43
Coolidge Dam, 29–30, 42–43
Corkum, L.V., 115
Cotton Marketing Cooperative for California and Arizona, 170
Cox, James, 23

Dague, Glenn, 47–49
death penalty, 54–55, 73, 77–78
Delbridge, Billie, 54
Democratic National Committee, 23, 39, 84, 106–7, 134–35
disbarment, 35–37
Douglas, Lewis, 153
Duffield, E.H., 92–96
Dugan, Eva, 50–55, 73, 77–79, 82–83
Dupa, Darrell, 19
Dust Bowl, 69–70

Eisenhower, Dwight D., 151–53, 189–90

8th Amendment, 82

Fannin, Paul, 161–63
Favorite, Jim, 19
Federal Communications Commission (FCC), 179
Federal Home Loan Bank of San Francisco, 156
FHA loans, 130
5th Amendment, 82, 166
fifth columnists, 123–24, 133–34
fishing, 113–14
Florence, AZ, 27, 31, 38–40, 42–43, 47–49
Fremon, John C., 19–20
Fulbright, Thomas, 41–49, 57, 66, 77, 83, 158

Gadsden Purchase, 27
Gardner, Ace, 49
GI Bill, 140, 189, 191
Gila River, 26, 29–30, 42–43, 49, 131, 185–86
Goddard, Sam, 163
Gold, Frank, 108–9
Goldwater, Barry, 90, 147, 150–55, 157, 161
Gordon, Frank X., 111
Graham, Elmer, 109
Great Depression, 31, 68, 70–71, 77, 84, 128–30, 161
Great Recession, 70–71
Green, E.L., 78, 81, 83
Griffin, Horace, 157
Gust, John L., 29

Hackley, Ivy, 155
Hall, William G., 88
Halloran, Jack, 74
Hammen, Melton Lawrence, 34–35
Harding, Warren G., 23, 121
Hayden, Carl, 99, 130–31, 139
Hearst, William Randolph, 75–77
Hill, Lister, 146
Hohokam, 26, 30–31, 131

Holmes, Richard, 183
Homeowner's Loan Act, 130
homesteading, 7, 27, 45
Hoover, Herbert, 67, 69–71, 128–30
Hoover Dam, 67–68, 114
Hunt, George W.P., 29, 54, 83–84, 99

Initiative and Reform, 24
Interstate Commerce Committee (ICC), 177
Interstate Oil Compact, 156
isolationism, 70–72, 92–94, 119, 134–35

Jacks, Maston, 127
Jencks, Joseph S., 77
Jennings, Irving, 110, 125–26, 135, 139, 141, 161–62
Jennings, Renz, 161–62
Johnson, Edwin, 146
Johnson, Lyndon Baines, 147–48, 155, 157, 176, 189, 191
Jones, Anthony, 145
Jones, Gerald, 52
Jones, Ross, 151–52
Judd, William C., 74
Judd, Winnie Ruth, 74–82

Karz, Edwin, 103
Kelly, Henry C., 109
Kerr, Robert S., 11
Kleindienst, Richard, 163
Korean War, 151–54
KTVK, 158, 177–80

Lake Mead, 114
LaPrade, Arthur T., 104
Larson, Mildred, 145
Lassen v. Arizona Highway Department, 165–66
Lehman, Hubert H., 146
LeRoi, Agnes, 74, 76
Lewis, Bill, 158, 168–70, 175, 193
Lewis, Del, 158, 172–73, 193

Lewis, Del, Jr., 158, 168, 193
Lewis, Jewell McFarland, 9, 87, 137, 151, 155, 158–59, 168–76, 180, 185, 192–93
Lewis, John L., 130, 158, 168–70, 173–74, 179, 181–82, 193
Lewis, Kara, 158, 168, 175–76, 193
Lewis, Leah, 158, 168, 172, 193
Lockwood, Alfred C., 35
Lockwood, Lorna, 77, 164

Magnuson, Warren, 146
Maricopa County, 27–28, 39, 49, 77
Marrow, Joe, 33
Mathis, Andrew J., 50–52
McCarran, Pat, 146
McCarthy, Joseph, 151
McCormack, John W., 169–70
McFarland, Carl, 10, 34–35, 61
McFarland, Clare Collins Smith: children of, 57–58, 64–66, 150–51, 182, 184–86; concerns for, 63; death of, 64, 150–51, 182, 184–86; Edna Smith McFarland and, 87; Ernest William McFarland and, 56–57; European trip of, 57–62, 139; as teacher, 56
McFarland, Edna Smith, 87–88, 137–38, 151, 155, 185, 193
McFarland, Ernest William (Mac): 1940 Democratic Senate primary and, 9, 93–96, 98–104; 1940 Democratic Senate primary lawyer letters of, 108–11; 1940 Democratic Senate primary voter letters of, 112–18; 1940 Senate election letter campaign of, 126–27; 1940 U.S. Senate election and, 125; 1952 U.S. Senate election and, 150–55; American Indian and, 8, 27, 43; as assistant attorney general, 29; autobiography of, 150–51, 184–85, 192; as a bank teller, 20; Barry Goldwater and, 150–55; birth of, 9, 187; campaign strategies of, 99–102, 105–7, 126–27, 162–63; as a Chief Justice,

160–67, 180, 191, 193; childhood of, 9–11; children of, 57–58, 64–66, 126, 150–51, 182, 184–86; clerking and, 23, 33; communications and, 177–78; conscription and, 102–3, 120–21; as a county attorney, 42–44, 115–16, 126, 191; death of, 180, 187; death of Franklin Delano Roosevelt and, 178–79; description of, 63; as district attorney, 28–29; early history of, 187; Edna Smith McFarland and, 87–90; education issues and, 115–16, 168–69, 174–75; education of, 10–12, 20–24, 39, 83, 98, 126, 133, 144; European trip of, 57–62, 139–41, 154–55; family of, 18, 97; farming and, 9, 32, 113–14, 122–23, 126, 133, 143–44, 158, 169, 188; father of, 7–10, 34–35; Florence, AZ and, 29–30; foreign policy and, 145–46; form letters of, 113–14; George W.P. Hunt and, 29; as goodwill ambassador, 154–55; as Governor, 9, 156–57, 190–91; grandchildren of, 26–27, 158–59, 168–76, 179, 193; Harry S. Truman and, 153; Henry Fountain Ashurst and, 93–97, 99–104; hunters and, 113–14; illness of, 15–18, 65, 185, 188; Jewell McFarland Lewis and, 9, 87, 151, 155, 171; as a judge, 9, 28, 55, 67, 69–70, 83–86, 115–16, 126, 191, 193; KTVK and, 158, 177–80; labor issues and, 130–31; law school and, 12–13, 20–24, 33–34, 83, 98, 126, 144; as a lawyer, 22–23, 33, 157, 193; legal opinions of, 166–67; as a lobbyist, 155; as majority leader, 146–47, 190–91; memorial to, 181–82; mother of, 7, 9–10, 17, 23, 34–35; move to Arizona by, 17–19; move to Washington D.C., 137–38; negative campaigning and, 99–102, 117–18; open-mindedness of, 63; perceptions of, 9–12, 100, 127–28, 133, 139–40, 142–43, 146–48, 167, 182, 188–89, 191–92; personality of, 7, 11–12, 22; physical description of, 14, 127; picture of, 10; Pinal County, AZ and, 9; political career of, 98; political science and, 22–23; poverty and, 128–29; preparedness and, 102–3, 133–35; as presidential material, 188–89; as private person, 88–89; as a public speaker, 11; radio and, 121–23, 126–27; retirement of, 166–67, 180; reversals of, 165–66; sanity trials and, 53–54, 77–83; as a Senator, 9, 22, 145–49, 189–91, 193; Social Security Act and, 132; sociology and, 22–23; speeches of, 128; as a teacher, 11, 187, 193; thesis of, 24–25; Thomas Fulbright and, 41; tragedies of, 57–58, 64–66, 126, 150–51, 182, 184–86; travels of, 32, 57–63, 140–41, 159, 168–70; as trustworthy, 148–49; use of media by, 118–24, 126–27; as a U.S. Navy Reservist, 17; U.S. Senate and, 98; water law and, 23–25, 29–30, 32, 114, 126, 133, 155; World War I service of, 13–17

McFarland, Etta Pearl, 7, 10, 34–35, 61
McFarland, Forrest, 7, 10, 34–35
McFarland, Jean Clare, 57, 64, 193
McFarland, Juliet, 64, 193
McFarland, Keziah Smith, 7, 10, 17, 23, 34–35
McFarland, William Ernest, 57, 64, 193
McFarland, William Thomas, 7–10, 34–35
McFarland Restoration Fund, 169
McKeller, Kenneth, 146
McKinnell, Burton, 75
McMillan, Jim, 29, 39, 56–57, 63, 88, 97, 101, 127–28, 145, 158, 161, 165–66, 178
Media America Communications, Inc. (MAC), 171–72, 180
Messenger, 103, 127
Meyers, Charles, 167
Miller, Lou, 110

Miller, Robert, 103
Mills, Rye, 45–46
mining, 27–28, 31, 115–16, 132
Miranda v. Arizona, 165–66
Mofford, Rose, 191
Moran, John, 167
Mormon Flat Dam, 29, 37
Mormon Lake, 90–91
Morrow, William M., 33
Murdock, John, 141
Murphy, James, 35–36
Murphy, John W., 29, 39, 116, 119
Murray, Porter, 81
Murray, Vince, 169, 183
Myrland, Otto, 52

Nash, J.F, 52
National Banking Law, 130
National Commission on the Causes and Prevention of Violence, 156
Naval Station Great Lakes, 14
Nazism, 133–34
New Deal, 31, 68, 84, 125, 130
1938 Presidential election, 69–70
1940 Democratic Senate primary, 9, 68, 93–96, 98–104
1940 U.S. Senate election, 125, 161
1952 U.S. Senate election, 150–55, 189
1964 Presidential election, 157, 163

O'Connor, Herbert, 146
O'Connor, J.E., 28
Oklahoma, 7–9, 34–35
organized labor, 125, 130, 132
Osborn, Sidney, 141

Parson, Wyly, 145
patriotism, 117, 135
Paul, Brady, 47–49
Pearl Harbor, 69–70, 172
Phillips, John Calhoun, 53
Pima River, 27
Pinal County, AZ, 9, 27–30, 39, 42–43, 45

Postal, 177–78
Pottawatomie Strip land run, 7–8, 143
Powers, Charlie, 145
Pulliam, Eugene, 152–53
Pyle, Howard, 151–52, 155

Ramirez, Esteban, 27
Rayburn, Sam, 148, 178–79
Reclamation Act of 1902, 131
Reclamation Service, 131
Republican National Committee, 106–7, 125, 135–36, 151–53
Rhodes, John, 151–52
Riggins, J.A., 109–10
River Cotton Gin, 170
Roosevelt, Franklin Delano, 67, 69–71, 84, 105–6, 122, 125–26, 132–35, 140–41, 178–79
Roosevelt, Theodore, 14, 141
Roosevelt Dam, 30
Ross, Frank E., 139–44
Ross, Henry, 77
Ryden, Don, 169, 182

Salt River, 131
Salt River Valley Users' Association (SRP), 29, 37
Samuelson, Hedvig, 74–75
Samuelson, Stanley, 52
San Carlos Dam, 29
San Carlos Irrigation and Drainage District, 30–31, 122
Santa Fe Colorado River, 111
Schroeder, Irene, 47–49
Scruggs, Edward W., 162–63
Seminole Nation, 9
Shadegg, Stephan, 153
Silverman, Dick, 164–65
Smith, Alexander, 146–47
Smith, Ann Collins, 56–57
Smith, Claude, 52
Smith, Poliet, 18–19
socialism, 153

Social Security Act, 132–33
sociology, 22–23
Spanish Influenza, 16
Speakerman, Howard, C., 75
Spires, Joe, 43–44, 59
SS George Washington, 61–62, 139
Stanford University, 21–22, 33–34, 39, 56, 83, 126
Stevenson, Adlai, 189–90
Stockton, Henderson, 103–4, 117–18
Struckmeyer, Fred, Jr., 164, 167
Summers, Harry, 28
Swilling, Jack, 19

Taft, Robert A., 178
tariffs, 101, 132
telegraph industry, 177–78
Tewksbury, George W., 117
Theilmann, R.H., 111
Tiger Woman, 47–49
Truman, Bill, 86
Truman, Harry S., 151–53, 178–79

Udall, Levi Stuart, 109, 164
"Unholy Three," 47–49
US Supreme Court, 157, 159, 165–66

Verde River, 131

Walsh, Jim, 145
Waters, Dick, 150–52
Western Union, 177–78
Wheeler, Burton K., 177
White, Scott, 54
White, William Allen, 84
Wilke, Wendell, 125–26, 141
Wilmer, Mark, 167
Woodward, Frederic Campbell, 21–22
World War I, 13, 45, 61–62, 71, 74, 92
World War II, 71, 92–95, 102, 106–7, 109, 119, 121, 126, 135–36, 143, 152, 177, 179
Wright, Lee, 48–49
Wynn, Bernie, 167

About the Author

Gary L. Stuart spent thirty years as a litigation partner at Jennings, Strouss & Salmon, PLLC, in Phoenix, Arizona. He now practices law part time as Gary L. Stuart, PC. He earned degrees in finance and law at the University of Arizona and served as notes editor on the *Arizona Law Review* and as president of *Phi Alpha Delta* legal fraternity. Martindale-Hubble lists him as an A-V lawyer and a Premier American Lawyer. He was profiled in *Who's Who in American Law* (first edition). He is an elected member of Best Lawyers in America, Arizona's Finest Lawyers, and Southwest Super Lawyers. He served as president and CEO of Arizona's Finest Lawyers, LLC, and is the current president of Arizona's Finest Lawyers Foundation, a nonprofit corporation. The Maricopa County Bar Association inducted him into its hall of fame in October 2010. The National Institute of Trial Advocacy honored him with its distinguished faculty designation in 1994. He holds the juried rank of advocate in and served as president of the American Board of Trial Advocates. Stuart completed an eight-year term on the Arizona Board of Regents and served as its president in 2004 and 2005. He taught as adjunct faculty at the University of Arizona James E. Rogers College of Law (2000–2005). He has been on the adjunct faculty at Arizona State University's Sandra Day O'Connor College of Law since 1994, where he continues to teach legal ethics, legal writing, and appellate advocacy. He also serves as senior policy advisor to the dean at the ASU College of Law and as vice president and general counsel of the *Arizona Legal Center*. He limits his part-time law practice to legal ethics, bar admission, professional discipline, law firm consulting, and expert witness work in legal malpractice and ethics cases. He served three terms on the Arizona State Bar's Case Conflict Committee as its probable cause panelist and was a charter member of the Arizona Supreme Court's Attorney Disciplinary Panel. He was a member of the Arizona State Bar Rules of Professional Conduct Committee for twenty-three years and served as its chair for ten years. He wrote more than State Bar Ethics Committee opinions. He served on numerous ethics-related committees at the state and national levels.

He wrote two published books on ethics, more than one hundred law review and journal articles, op-ed pieces, essays, stories, and CLE monographs. His ten published books are: *The Ethical Trial Lawyer* (State Bar of Arizona, 1994); *Litigation Ethics* (Lexis-Nexis Publishing, 1998); *The Gallup 14: A Novel* (University of New Mexico Press, 2000); *Miranda—The Story of America's Right to Remain Silent* (University of Arizona Press, 2004); *AIM For The Mayor—Echoes from Wounded Knee: A Novel* (Xlibris Publishing, 2008); *Innocent Until Interrogated—The Story of the Buddhist Temple Massacre and the Tucson Four* (University of Arizona Press, 2010); *Ten Shoes Up: A Novel* (Gleason & Wall Publishing, 2015); *The Valles Caldera: A Novel* (Gleason & Wall Publishing, 2015); *Anatomy of A Confession—The Debra Milke Case* (ABA Publishing, 2016); *The Last Stage to Bosque Redondo: A Novel* (Gleason & Wall Publishing, 2017).